WORKING WITH INDIGENOUS KNOWLEDGE

A GUIDE FOR RESEARCHERS

Louise Grenier

INTERNATIONAL DEVELOPMENT RESEARCH CENTRE

Ottawa • Cairo • Dakar • Johannesburg • Montevideo • Nairobi • New Delhi • Singapore

Published by the International Development Research Centre
PO Box 8500, Ottawa, ON, Canada K1G 3H9

© International Development Research Centre 1998

Legal deposit: 1st quarter 1998
National Library of Canada
ISBN 0-88936-847-3

The catalogue of IDRC Books may be consulted online at
http://www.idrc.ca/index_e.html

Contents

Acknowledgments

A very rough draft of this guidebook was compiled for a workshop on indigenous technical knowledge funded by the International Development Research Centre (IDRC) and the Ford Foundation, and held in Hanoi, Vietnam, in November 1996. I owe many thanks to Stephen Tyler, IDRC Singapore, who not only hired me to deliver the workshop, but subsequently encouraged me to develop the materials for publication.

At IDRC Ottawa, Chusa Gines reviewed and approved the materials for publication for the Sustainable Use of Biodiversity Program — *muchos gracias* to Chusa for coordinating and managing the publication process. I must thank Fred Carden, Bill Carman, Sam Landon, Stephen Langill, and Erin O'Manique, also from IDRC, for their insights and helpful comments on the draft.

I am particularly grateful to the following reviewers for lending their expertise, ideas, criticism, wisdom, and editorial insights to the draft: Andrew J. Satterthwaite, York University; Frank J. Tester, the School of Social Work at The University of British Columbia; and Ian M. Whelan, Program Director, Cultural Survival Canada. You have taught me so much.

This guidebook also owes its existence to the hard work and intellectual contributions of a considerable number of other individuals — in particular, all those people cited in my reference list. Although the views expressed in this guide reflect my interpretation and synthesis, the referenced experiences greatly complemented, challenged, or made complete my own experiences on the topic of indigenous knowledge.

Last, special thanks go to the Giroux family: Danielle, François, Nathalie, Chantal, and Michelle. My sister's family was there to witness the ups and downs of getting this publication together. I owe you all for your patience and assistance.

Louise Grenier
November 1997

Introduction

Why work *with* indigenous knowledge (IK)? In an article on sustainability and technology transfer, Richard Wilk (1995), an American anthropologist, mentioned a file folder of materials that he had accumulated over several years. The file contained 25 separate project proposals, feasibility studies, implementation plans, and project assessments. Submitted over a period of a century, all these studies considered commercializing the production of edible palm oil from a tree native to the Belizean rainforest. In each of these initiatives, imported cracking and rendering technologies developed for use in other tropical palm-oil industries were tried. Despite easy access to dense, high-yield tree stands, all these projects failed, even those with direct government subsidies. Throughout this period, household production of edible oil by indigenous people, using a variety of simple, local technologies, never stopped.

This story prompts several important questions: Did anyone bother to ask local people the who, how, where, when, and why of their local palm-oil production system? By learning about the local production system, could the proponents have avoided any of these costly failures? If the entrepreneurs had established joint ventures with the communities, could development objectives and sustainable-development goals have been served? If participatory technology-development techniques had been tried, could hybrid technologies (a combination of indigenous and foreign inputs) have yielded successful ventures? What would have been the outcome had any of these proponents worked *with* IK?

The experiences of an agroforestry project in the Philippines, initiated by the International Institute of Rural Reconstruction, suggests that outcomes can be quite different. After a nursery operation that relied on exotic species failed to live up to expectations, village farmers and scientists worked together to identify locally growing (indigenous and introduced) tree species. Local informants identified the most important species, listed the criteria used for classifying a species as "important" — hardiness, fire resistance, general utility, and seed availability — and then ranked the species according to the criteria. Six indigenous and four exotic species were identified as having significant potential as new nursery stock, according to these criteria. The results of this exercise were presented to the whole community, and the community now has its own action plan for reforestation. Scientists and farmers learned from each other, and local people were empowered (IIRR 1996).

A decade ago, there was very little research that focused on IK, and there were even fewer examples of successful IK-based interventions. But since the early 1990s, IK has been fertile ground for research. With so much activity, there is now a wealth of information on the topic — in fact, lots of "pieces" of information all over the place. Because IK research is still relatively new, comprehensive source materials are rare. This guidebook specifically addresses that need: it gathers and integrates information on the topic, making a whole package of information accessible, comprehensible, and hence, useful. Through extensive use of field examples and a review of current theory and practice, it provides a succinct and comprehensive overview of IK research and assessment.

By summarizing an extensive literature (including the research results from foreign and local researchers) and presenting some key positions brought forward by indigenous peoples, this guide contributes to the improved design, delivery, monitoring, and evaluation of research programs in indigenous peoples' territories. Two audiences are anticipated: seasoned development-intervention professionals, project managers, research coordinators, and extensionists seeking to add some insights and options to their development approaches; and the novice or student needing an informative sourcebook on IK or a framework for further study.

In the sections that follow, methods of incorporating IK systems in development work are discussed. Section 1 serves as general introduction to the topic. To explain why IK deserves our attention today, this section concludes with a short discussion on sustainable development. Section 2 addresses some of the ethical issues in IK research. Intellectual property rights and the emerging ethical, legal, and commercial contexts affecting IK research are discussed. Section 3 looks at research paradigms, briefly mapping out insights generated from the International Union for the Conservation of Nature and Natural Resources framework for assessing progress toward sustainability, the social sciences, and gender-sensitive and participatory rural research. This section concludes by tabulating all inputs as one framework (see Table 3). Section 4 expands on the topic of IK methodology by offering details on 31 field techniques. Section 5 presents four case studies, demonstrating different approaches to IK research in terms of research objectives and collection techniques. Section 6 deals with assessing the product of IK research in terms of sustainability and looks at developing IK through validation and experimentation. Three sets of formal procedural guidelines for conducting IK research are presented in Appendix 1. The guidelines can be adapted to other situations. A glossary of the terms that are in **_bold italics_** and a list of acronyms and abbreviations are included as Appendix 2 and Appendix 3, respectively.

What about Indigenous Knowledge?

Some characteristics of IK

For the purpose of this guidebook, *indigenous knowledge* (IK) refers to the unique, traditional, local knowledge existing within and developed around the specific conditions of women and men indigenous to a particular geographic area. (It is acknowledged that nonindigenous people, in particular people living off the land, have their own indigenous or local knowledge, but this topic is not addressed here.) The development of IK systems, covering all aspects of life, including management of the natural environment, has been a matter of survival to the peoples who generated these systems. Such knowledge systems are cumulative, representing generations of experiences, careful observations, and trial-and-error experiments.

> When a knowledgeable old person dies, a whole library disappears.
>
> *An old African proverb*

IK systems are also dynamic: new knowledge is continuously added. Such systems do innovate from within and also will internalize, use, and adapt external knowledge to suit the local situation.

All members of a community have *traditional ecological knowledge:* elders, women, men, and children. The quantity and quality of the IK that individuals possess vary. Age,

> Ruddle (1993) examined the transmission of traditional ecological knowledge for sites in Venezuela and Polynesia. Two- to five-year-old children already knew the names and characteristics of the more common biota. By the age of 14, children were competent in household tasks, cultivation (plant identification, harvesting), seed selection, weeding, animal husbandry, fishing, and hunting. Overall, he found that the training was age specific, structured, and systematic. Specific times are allocated to training during the daily work routine.

education, *gender,* social and economic status, daily experiences, outside influences, roles and responsibilities in the home and community, profession, available time, aptitude and intellectual capability, level of curiosity and observation skills, ability to travel and degree of autonomy, and control over natural resources are some of the influencing factors.

IK is stored in peoples' memories and activities and is expressed in stories, songs, folklore, proverbs, dances, myths, cultural values, beliefs, rituals, community laws, local language and taxonomy, agricultural practices, equipment, materials, plant species, and animal breeds. IK is shared and communicated orally, by specific example, and through culture. Indigenous forms of communication and organization are vital to local-level decision-making processes and to the preservation, development, and spread of IK.

What is included in IK research?

Although each IK system consists of an integrated body of knowledge, researchers interested in learning more about traditional knowledge systems tend to focus on discrete aspects. A diversity of topics are studied under the rubric of IK research. To convey an appreciation of the scope of the research area, examples are listed below.

- *Learning systems* — indigenous methods of imparting knowledge; indigenous approaches to innovation and experimentation; indigenous games; and indigenous specialists;

- *Local organizations, controls, and enforcement* — traditional institutions for environmental management; common-property management practices; traditional decision-making processes; conflict-resolution practices; traditional laws, rights, taboos, and rituals; and community controls on harvesting;

- *Local classification and quantification* — a community's definitions and classification of phenomena and local flora and fauna; and indigenous methods of counting and quantifying;

> The Inuit classify mammals according to whether they are sea or land animals: *puijiit* are those that rise to the surface, and *pisutiit* are those that walk.
>
> *Source: Nakashima (1990)*

- *Human health* — nutrition; human-disease classification systems; traditional medicine and the use of herbal remedies in treatment of diseases; and the locations of medicinal plants, the proper times for collection, the most useful parts, and the methods for preparing and storing medicines;

- *Animals and animal diseases* — animal breeding and production; traditional fodder and forage species and their specific uses; animal-disease classification; and traditional ethnoveterinary medicine;

- *Water* — traditional water-management and water-conservation systems; traditional techniques for irrigation; use of specific species for water conservation; and freshwater and saltwater fisheries and aquatic-resource management;

- *Soil* — soil conservation practices; the use of specific species for soil conservation; and soil-fertility enhancement practices;

- *Agriculture* — indigenous indicators to determine favourable times to prepare, plant, and harvest gardens; land-preparation practices; indigenous ways to propagate plants; seed storage and processing (drying, threshing, cleaning, and grading); seed practices; indigenous methods of sowing (seed spacing and intercropping); seedling preparation and care; farming and cropping systems (for example, complementary groupings); crop harvesting and storage; food processing and marketing; and pest-management systems and plant- protection methods;

> Rats cause serious losses in coconuts, so the local people on Maldivian atolls wrap large palm leaves around the tree trunks, effectively preventing rats from climbing the trees.
>
> *Source: Hunter (1996)*

- *Agroforestry and swidden agriculture* — indigenous techniques used for recognizing potential swidden farmland and the criteria used for making choices regarding its use; criteria and techniques used for allowing a farm to go fallow; fallow management and uses; indigenous adaptations for intensification; changes adopted during the shift to sedentary agriculture; the management of forest plots and the productivity of forest plots; the knowledge and use of forest plants (and animals); and the interrelationship between tree species, improved crop yields, and soil fertility; and

- *Other topics* — textiles and other local crafts; building materials; energy conversion; indigenous tools; and changes to local systems over time.

The erosion of IK systems

As outsiders have become increasingly aware of the value of IK, so has the awareness that IK systems, *biodiversity,* and cultural diversity (three interacting, interdependent systems) are threatened with extinction. Notwithstanding the fact that some IK is lost naturally as techniques and tools are modified or fall out of use, the recent and current rate of loss is accelerating because of rapid population growth, growth of international markets, educational systems, environmental

> "We are reminded of the global and historical tendency of complex technologies associated with economic powers to squash smaller, local technologies... We are urged to identify the valuable elements of smaller technologies and to create a place for them in the new century."
>
> *Source: Kroma (1996)*

degradation, and development processes — pressures related to rapid modernization and cultural homogenization. Below, some examples are given to illustrate these mechanisms:

- With rapid population growth — often due to in-migration or government relocation schemes in the case of large development projects, such as dams — standards of living may be compromised. With poverty, opportunities for short-term gain are selected over environmentally sound local practices. With increasing levels of poverty, farmers, for example, may also have less time and fewer resources to sustain the dynamic nature of IK systems through their local experiments and innovations.

- The introduction of market-oriented agricultural and forestry practices focused on monocropping is associated with losses in IK and IK practices, through losses in biodiversity and cultural diversity. For instance, policies promoting generic rice and wheat varieties devalue locally adapted species.

> An elderly woman in northern India was selecting seeds for storage while being interviewed by a researcher about the impacts of modern agriculture. She commented, "It takes a sharp eye, a sensitive hand, and a lot of patience to tell the difference between these seeds. These are not the things that are honoured any more."
>
> *Source: Zweifel (1997)*

- With the ready availability of many commercial foods, some biodiversity *seems* to become less relevant, such as seed and crop varieties selected over the years for their long-term storage attributes.

- In the short term, chemical inputs *seem* to reduce the need to tailor varieties to difficult growing conditions, contributing to the demise of local varieties. (However, the failure of green-revolution technology strongly suggests that uniformity is a poor long-term strategy.)

- With deforestation, certain medicinal plants become more difficult to find (and the knowledge or culture associated with the plants also declines).

- More and more knowledge is being lost as a result of the disruption of traditional channels of oral communication. Neither children nor adults spend as much time in their communities anymore (for example, some people travel to the city on a daily basis to go to school, to look for work, or to sell farm produce; many young people are no longer interested in, or do not have the opportunity for, learning traditional methods). It is harder for the older generation to transmit their knowledge to young people.

- Because IK is transmitted orally, it is vulnerable to rapid change — especially when people are displaced or when young people acquire values and lifestyles different from those of their ancestors.

- Farmers traditionally maintained their indigenous crop varieties by keeping household seed stocks and by obtaining seed through traditional family and community networks and through exchanges with nearby communities. Some of these traditional networks have been disrupted or no longer exist.

In the past, outsiders (for example, social, physical, and agricultural scientists, biologists, colonial powers) ignored or maligned IK, depicting it as primitive, simple, static, "not knowledge," or folklore. This historic neglect (regardless of its cause — racism, ethnocentrism, or modernism, with its complete faith in the scientific method) has contributed to the decline of IK systems, through lack of use and application. This legacy is still in evidence. Many professionals are still sceptical. Also, in some countries, official propaganda depicts indigenous cultures and methodologies as backward or out of date and simultaneously promotes one national culture and one language at the expense of minority cultures. Often, formal schooling reinforces this negative attitude. Local people's perceptions (or misperceptions) of local species and of their own traditional systems may need to be rebuilt. Some local people and communities have lost confidence in their ability to help themselves and have become dependent on external solutions to their local problems.

Why the sudden interest in IK?

The interest (of outsiders) in this "old" knowledge is recent and emerged in tandem with the politicization of indigenous groups and the indigenous-rights movements. Many indigenous peoples are demanding the right to be heard in development decisions. This often includes demanding that their rights to land and resources be recognized and officially acknowledged. Concurrently, the international political system and many national governments are showing some willingness to listen to indigenous peoples. In a sense, this improved political climate supports a dialogue on IK. Some governments (Australia, Canada, Greenland, the United States) have mechanisms such as settled land claims and comanagement resource boards that support IK systems by supporting self-government and the joint management of natural resources. (Although the settlement of land claims and other indigenous rights is considered a key facet of the recognition and legitimization of IK, the pressures of self-government and its financing have made it difficult for indigenous governments to develop using their own logic and wisdom [Tester, personal communication, 1997].[1])

> "Given enough time, everything that is old will become new again."
>
> *Source: Conway (1997)*

As well, the "life industry" (those industries that profit from the use of living organisms — agrochemical, pharmaceutical, food, and seed industries) and critics of the life industry have done much to reveal the past, current, and future value of IK and the implications for indigenous peoples of its unregulated theft from the South (see Section 2, "Protecting Intellectual Property Rights").

Of late, IK has been lauded as an "alternative collective wisdom relevant to a variety of matters at a time when existing norms, values and laws are increasingly called into question" (Berkes 1993, p. 7). The need for some alternative wisdom in development initiatives is supported by the following observations:

- Green-revolution technology is associated with ecological deterioration, economic decline (at the local level), and poorer diets and nutritional losses resulting from the eradication of traditional foods or from their substitution by nontraditional foods.

---

[1] F.J. Tester, School of Social Work, The University of British Columbia, Vancouver, BC, Canada, personal communication, 1997.

- Development as planned and implemented for the last 30 years has placed unprecedented pressures on the planet's soils, watersheds, forests, and other natural resources.

- Some development solutions from outside are based on incorrect assumptions, are not economically feasible or culturally acceptable, and are often abandoned (for example, techniques are too complex or require too much maintenance).

- Some technical solutions are introduced to solve problems not perceived at the local level and are abandoned.

- Development interventions tend to benefit small numbers of people from relatively privileged groups.

- Some critics observe that communities receiving the most externally driven development assistance become less capable of handling their own affairs.

- Top-down planning fails to promote effective natural-resource management at the local level.

In short, development planning has often failed to achieve the desired result: *sustainable development*. In some cases, "dependencies have been created by an outside world that orders and demands (through laws and natural resource regulations) but does not truly contribute to development. Communities are often left to find their own means" (de Vreede 1996).

Development efforts that ignore local circumstances, local technologies, and local systems of knowledge have wasted enormous amounts of time and resources. Compared with many modern technologies, traditional techniques have been tried and tested; are effective, inexpensive, locally available, and culturally appropriate; and in many cases are based on preserving and building on the patterns and processes of nature.

> Some farmers in Zimbabwe prefer to use a local strategy to combat termites and ants, rather than the commercial remedy, which is expensive and not readily available. Termites are the major destroyers of gum and orchard trees, especially during the early stages of growth. Through their informal experiments, the farmers discovered that either ashes or a mix of a small smelly plant ground together with onions and paraffin or used oil repels termites and ants.
>
> *Source: Hanyani-Mlambo and Hebinck (1996)*

Western technoscientific approaches are (in themselves) an insufficient response to today's complex web of social, economic, political, and environmental challenges. The paradigm in support of "one technology or one knowledge system fits all" has been debunked. IK systems suggest a different approach to problem solving. Whereas Western science attempts to isolate a problem — to eliminate its interlinkage with various other factors and to reduce a problem to a small number of controllable parameters — traditional approaches usually examine problems in their entirety, together with their interlinkages and complexities (Shankar 1996). For example, people in the field of medicine are realizing the importance of including the physical, spiritual, sociocultural, and psychological well-being of a person when considering matters of health. Although this is a fairly new concept for modern medicine, this holistic approach is the basis of many traditional systems.

> "Ecosystems sustain themselves in a dynamic balance based on cycles and fluctuations, which are non-linear processes. Ecological awareness, then, will arise only when we combine our rational knowledge with an intuition for the non-linear nature of our environment. Such intuitive wisdom is characteristic of traditional, non-literate cultures... in which life was organized around a highly refined awareness of environment."
>
> *Source: Capra (1982), cited in Berkes (1993, p. 1)*

Increasingly, development practitioners argue that paying attention to local IK can

- Create mutual respect, encourage local participation, and build partnerships for joint problem resolution;

- Facilitate the design and implementation of culturally appropriate development programs, avoiding costly mistakes;

- Identify techniques that can be transferred to other regions;

- Help identify practices suitable for investigation, adaptation, and improvement; and

- Help build a more sustainable future.

IK for sustainable development

Sustainable development is "development that meets the needs of the present without compromising the ability of future generations to meet their own needs" (WCED 1987, p. 43). Sustainable agricultural and natural-resource development means "the utilization, management and conservation of the natural resource base and the orientation of technological change to ensure the attainment and continued satisfaction of human needs — such as food,

water, shelter, clothing and fuel — for present and future generations"
(Titilola 1995).

According to the World Commission on Environment and
Development, sustainable development has the following nine objectives
(WCED 1987):

- Reviving growth;

- Changing the quality of growth;

- Meeting essential needs for jobs, food, energy, water, and sanitation;

- Ensuring a sustainable level of population;

- Conserving and enhancing the resource base;

- Reorienting technology and managing risk;

- Merging environmental considerations and economics in decision-
  making;

- Reorienting international economic relations; and

- Making development more participatory.

Sustainable development at the local and national levels is a function
of five variables (Matowanyika 1991):

- Biophysical and socioeconomic resources;

- External factors, such as available technologies and development
  ideologies;

- Internal factors, including sociocultural belief systems and local production and technological bases;

- Population factors; and

- Political and economic factors.

A sustainable-development strategy will take into account all of the
above variables and will involve working, learning, and experimenting
together at the local, regional, national, and international levels. The predom-
inant focus of this guidebook is on the local level and what IK can contribute
to a local sustainable-development strategy, taking into account local circumstances, potential, experiences, and wisdom.

Sustainable development at the local level is dependent on the implementation of enabling mechanisms at the local, national, and international

How is IK used in Canada?

IK improves scientific research

Canada's indigenous populations are helping to improve scientific research programs. For instance, in a whale-tagging program involving local people, traditional knowledge solved problems with the methods being used to tag the whales. New tagging techniques developed with local people were very successful (AINA and JS–IRRC 1996).

IK is used to provide environmental baseline data

IK is increasingly used to provide environmental baseline data for environmental-impact assessments. For instance, scientific understanding of Canada's vast eastern Arctic ecosystem remains severely limited. Fortunately, Inuit hunters know the life histories, population dynamics, migration patterns, and spatial and temporal distributions of the wildlife. This information is necessary for completing wildlife inventories and for assessing and predicting the potential impacts of development options. It should be noted that indigenous peoples' population estimates of caribou, fish, or whale populations have been found to be far more accurate than scientific estimates. Also, areas identified as "critical" by scientists are not always the same as those identified by residents.

IK is used as a decision-making tool in environmental-impact assessments

The Nunavut Land Claim Agreement comes into effect in 1999, at which time the Inuit will govern Canada's vast eastern Arctic. The procedures for the Nunavut Impact Review Board specify that IK is to be considered as being (at least) equal to scientific knowledge. In short, if local people do not support a development option, the Board will likely reject or modify the development proposal. In other areas of northern Canada, government and proponents show some commitment to using local people's traditional ecological knowledge to suggest project-site alternatives or measures to avoid or reduce long- and short-term damage to the ecosystem and traditional culture.

IK is used to monitor development impacts

IK has an important impact-monitoring role during the life of a project and for the postproject period. Local people are familiar with the natural variability of their environment and are more likely to be able to distinguish on-going (natural) environmental changes from project-induced changes. Most scientists are not in a position to obtain this type of information themselves. Aboriginal people often notice minor changes in environmental health (in the quality, odour, and vitality of environmental components) long before government enforcement agencies, scientists, or other observers (Wavey 1993). For example, the Manitoba Keewatinowi Okimakanak and the Environmental Protection Laboratories jointly designed a water-quality sampling program near a copper–zinc mine. The program was developed because local people were refusing to eat the wildlife and to drink the water near the mine; they had noted a change in taste in the meat and water (Sallenave 1994).

levels, which is beyond the scope of this discussion. At the local level, people need additional resources and more control over their local resources. Land users need secure land and resource tenure — to encourage the local reinvestment of profits — and economic policies that improve terms of trade vis-à-vis large-scale markets. Local people also need to participate in and influence those decision-making processes by which they are affected. Appropriate authority will need to devolve from national and subnational government to local government. At the international level, enabling global agreements and trade patterns and a reduction in foreign-debt obligations are needed (Krugmann 1996).

> The main strength of traditional practices for sustainable development is that they have evolved in close contact with specific cultural and environmental conditions. Certain traditional techniques have proved to be sustainable in the sense that they have given good results over a long period, for example, the irrigation schemes of Bali. Traditional methods, however, do not guarantee sustainability. Slash-and-burn agriculture, for instance, can become unsustainable when cultivated areas do not lie fallow long enough for soil regeneration to take place (e.g., where large populations have been relocated). So, the dichotomy of "modern = unsustainable and traditional = sustainable" is overly simplistic.
>
> *Source: Zwahlen (1996)*

It should also be noted that incorporating IK into current development practice and applying it to the problem of sustainability is not without some risk to indigenous peoples. Most notably, there is usually a big difference between the power wielded by indigenous peoples and that wielded by outside parties. IK can be applied to the problem of sustainability or it can be applied to the dominant paradigm, furthering the problems of an unsustainable world through its (mis)use by, for instance, transnational corporations (TNCs) (Tester, personal communication,1997, see p. 6).

Protecting Intellectual Property Rights

Intellectual property rights

Intellectual property rights (IPR) are mechanisms to protect individual and industrial "inventions" and are usually in effect for a specified period. These legal rights can be attached to information if the information can be applied to making a product that is distinctive and useful. Legal rights prevent others from copying, selling, or importing a product without authorization. In essence, there are six forms of intellectual property: patents, plant-breeders' rights, copyright, trademarks, industrial designs, and trade secrets. Patents and plant-breeders' rights are the two forms relevant to this discussion (RAFI 1996a).

To be eligible for a patent, inventions should be novel, nonobvious, and useful. In theory, intellectual property laws ensure that inventors and investors will be rewarded for their investments if their product is successfully commercialized. IPR mechanisms give patent-holders exclusive monopoly over their invention for 17–30 years and royalties on the use of their invention. IPR mechanisms also allow the patent-holder to control access to, or set the conditions for the sale of, the invention, as the patent-holder can vary the licencing arrangements. The patent-holder can also deny access to some customers. In practice, intellectual property regimes have evolved into mechanisms that allow corporations to protect markets and to trade technologies among themselves, barring smaller enterprises from entering the market (RAFI 1996a).

Patent laws were originally designed to protect factory machinery. Historically, technology-importing countries were reluctant to adopt patent laws, wanting to avoid paying royalties to other countries. Technology exporters, on the other hand, were anxious to take out patents in every country with a market (RAFI 1996a).

In the 1800s, most national patent laws in Europe excluded living materials, foods, and medicines from protection. Much has changed since then. Groups of living things first came under intellectual property with the US 1930 *Plant Patent Act,* which targeted some asexual plants. In the early 1960s, the United States passed a law granting plant breeders the right to patent seeds, preventing others from selling the same variety (Lehman 1994). Since 1980, when the US Supreme Court ruled that an oil-eating microbe was patentable, the trend has been to extend patent law to many life forms (Harry 1995b). The US Patent and Trademark Office ruled in 1985 that plants could qualify under industrial patent laws and, in 1987, that animals were patentable (RAFI 1996a). In the case of plant materials, patents can now be in effect for 17–30 years.

Currently, there are a number of IPR regimes in operation in Europe, the United States, and elsewhere. The newer laws tend to cover a broad spectrum of life forms and grant astonishing degrees of ownership to the

Genetic engineering

Biotechnology companies are interested in engineering crops that grow over a wider geographical range; herbicide-tolerant plants (allowing herbicides to be sprayed more often); foods that ripen more slowly (allowing food to be shipped farther); "pharm" plants and animals (living pharmaceutical factories); animals that grow faster and larger or have "desired" characteristics (for example, lean, fast-growing crippled pigs); and northern plants that produce products like cocoa or vanilla. Already, bio-engineered substitutes for crops such as sugar and plant oils are in the marketplace, threatening the economies of some developing countries (Meister and Mayer 1995).

Some engineered organisms may have unanticipated harmful impacts on other species and the environment. A case from Oregon State University illustrates that point (Dawkins et al. 1995). Scientists engineered bacteria to more efficiently convert agricultural wastes to ethanol fuel. Tests conducted late in the process (and fortunately before the microbe's release) determined that the new microbe destroyed a beneficial mycorrhizal fungus and thus could have prevented nearby plants from absorbing nitrogen, an essential nutrient .

Genetic-engineering technology remains largely unregulated: only a few states and Organisation for Economic Co-operation and Development countries have regulations governing the release of genetically engineered organisms (Harry 1995b). Many developing countries do not have such regulations. Unregulated releases and illegal releases of genetically engineered organisms have occurred, particularly in the South, and some companies appear to be using developing countries as their testing grounds (Meister and Mayer 1995). The Shiva Working Group on Global Sustainability advocates a worldwide moratorium on the release of genetically engineered organisms until strict regulations are in place covering their transfer, handling, and use, arguing that the threat of "genetic pollution" is real (SWGGS 1995a). Little public debate has taken place on the moral and ethical questions raised by genetic engineering: Are new life forms needed or desirable?

patent-holder. Moreover, when IPR laws are amended, the scope of protection and the rights of patent-holders tend to be expanded.

Countries such as Argentina, Brazil, and India have allowed patents on processes but not products and have compelled patent-holders to make socially useful products available in the domestic market (Dawkins et al. 1995). That approach has helped to insulate national economies from the global market and from the market monopolies of TNCs.

The US 1985 Utility Plant Patent is the most powerful protection available for plant and plant-related inventions. A single application may cover multiple varieties or even an entire genus or species. These plant patents can cover biological material, processes, genes, proteins, recombinant processes, culture techniques, plant parts, and seeds. For instance, patent-holders who identify new genes can claim 20 years of exclusive control over that gene in any plant, including derived seeds and tissue. The Utility Plant Patent is often used to cover genetically engineered materials — whether whole organisms, tissue cultures, cells, or DNA sequences — and transgenic materials.

Transgenic organisms

Transgenic materials are life forms created by transferring selected genes from one variety or species to another. There are now many transgenic organisms: rat genes have been transferred to pigs in an attempt to increase the pigs' reproductive capacity; a human gene has been transferred to bulls to see if next-generation cows produce human milk proteins (Davidman 1996); pig and chicken genes have been moved into plants (SWGGS 1995b). There are some concerns that transferred genes might carry with them the potential to cause allergic reactions or a resistance to antibiotics. With food items, the fear is that such resistance could be transferred to human beings (Davidman 1996). Labeling is not yet required on these products; thus, health, religious edicts, and food preferences such as vegetarianism may be compromised (SWGGS 1995b).

At the international level, the question of what is patentable is both unsettled and controversial. On 18 June 1997, the European Parliament Legal Affairs Committee voted to allow industry to have patents on living organisms, overturning its current patent law. Concerned groups are lobbying against the proposal, arguing that the proposal addresses only the interests of the biotechnology industry (Global 2000 1997).

Corporations are well aware of how cost efficient it is to tap the knowledge of communities that live with and depend on biodiversity for their survival. Pharmaceutical TNCs have taken plant samples from tropical forests (identified and genetically manipulated by indigenous peoples) to use as raw materials in developing new drugs. Agricultural companies took disease-resistant seeds (identified and genetically manipulated by indigenous peoples). After some modifications, this genetic material was patented, mainly in the United States, and the resulting seed or product was marketed. Moving a single gene from one spot to another within a cell, whether or not it causes an actual variation in the next generation, creates a sufficiently "new" plant variety to qualify as a patentable invention.

> The world market value of pharmaceuticals derived from plants used in traditional medicine had an estimated value of 43 billion United States dollars [USD] in 1985. Less than 0.001% of the profits has gone to the original holders of that knowledge.
>
> *Source: CS Canada (1995)*

Corporations have realized enormous benefits from their free access to genetic materials, especially in the case of crop plants from developing countries (Nowlan 1995).

The Convention on Biological Diversity

The 1992 Convention on Biological Diversity, a legally binding international agreement, was developed at the United Nations Conference on Environment and Development. It came into force in December 1993. The 150 signatories to the Convention made a commitment to "the conservation of biological diversity, the sustainable use of its components and the fair and equitable sharing of the benefits arising out of the utilization of genetic resources" (Article 1).

> When it was signed, the Convention did not apply to *ex situ* plant or microbe collections established before the Convention. Those extensive collections were deemed to belong to the people who had deposited the samples and not to the countries the materials had been taken from! Steps were taken to clarify the legal status of these collections, and in late 1994 all the materials in these gene banks were made the property of the Food and Agriculture Organization of the United Nations, which will place the collections under the Convention on Biological Diversity.
>
> *Source: RAFI (1996a)*

The Convention states that genetic resources, like mineral and oil resources, are subject to national legislation, meaning that nation states have a right to set conditions and limits on access to genetic resources. The Convention also states that access to genetic resources will be subject to "prior informed consent." This is consent given after a full account of the reasons for the activity, the specific procedures involved, the potential risks, and the foreseeable outcomes (Posey and Dutfield 1996).

To date, the benefits arising from the use of genetic resources have not been equitably shared, which contravenes Article 8(j) of the Convention

(Nowlan 1995). Only a few drug companies have started to make payments to some research institutes or governments. No benefits have been returned to indigenous communities (Davidman 1996). Although the Convention recognizes the importance of biological IK, more often than not this knowledge has been used without the approval and involvement of the holders of such knowledge (Nowlan 1995).

"The global food system is dependent on the expropriation of plant genetic materials from indigenous peoples' territories because biodiversity has been systematically eliminated wherever farmers adopt the large-scale, high-input, food production models championed by agribusiness corporations."

Source: CS Canada (1996c)

"Southern farmers cultivate the agricultural biodiversity that allows food crops to adapt to changes, whether evolving pests, diseases, climate change or human intervention. ... However, government policies and commercial pressures push farmers to replace their own varieties with high-tech, high-input, higher-yielding varieties of staple grains and livestock breeds."

Source: RAFI (1996a)

Although the Convention on Biological Diversity affirms the sovereignty of nations over their biological resources, it also accepts the concept of intellectual property over living things and encourages bilateral arrangements between those who want access to resources and knowledge (for example, corporations) and governments. The Convention does not define protection at the level of the community, thus setting the stage for intercommunity conflicts or conflicts between a government and its communities. Overall, the Convention lacks teeth: it has no mechanisms to control outsider's access to indigenous bioresources (for example, a binding code of conduct) and no mechanisms to determine the equitable sharing of benefits (RAFI 1996a).

The General Agreement on Tariffs and Trade

Until recently, intellectual property was subject to national legislation. Nations were free to determine whether and how they would recognize intellectual property. From a corporate standpoint, intellectual property laws in one country are of limited value without parallel

"Sweeping patent claims extending to any plant engineered to express a specific gene or to exhibit a particular trait demonstrate dramatically that the intellectual property system is recklessly out-of-control."

Source: RAFI (1995)

recognition by other countries. Accordingly, industrialized nations and corporations have lobbied aggressively to harmonize legislation at the international level.

The General Agreement on Tariffs and Trade (GATT), established in 1947, is an agreement to remove tariff and nontariff barriers to trade. In 1994, negotiators of the Uruguay Round agreement of the GATT established that member countries are to bring their national IPR laws into conformity with the new agreement on Trade-Related Aspects of Intellectual Property Rights (TRIPS). Effective 1 January 1995, TRIPS obliges member countries (now, more than 115 member states, of which 70 are from the South) to implement patent coverage for microorganisms and some form of IPR over plant varieties. Furthermore, members are given the option to exclude from coverage plants and animals other than microorganisms and the "essentially biological processes for the production of plants or animals other than non-biological and microbiological processes" (Dawkins et al. 1995).

TRIPS will protect products for 20 years, then extend protection for another 20 years to the manufacturing process if the process is new (Sayeed 1994). The South has until year 2000 and least-developed countries have until 2004 to either adopt an existing international IPR convention or develop their own (RAFI 1996a). The World Trade Organization (WTO), which is now responsible for GATT, will review IPR provisions in 1999, before any Southern government is required to enact legislation. Once adopted, these rules will replace national laws.

The United States has interpreted the provisions of the Convention on Biological Diversity as being subordinate to those of the GATT (Dawkins et al. 1995). How the TRIPS provisions are interpreted (and implemented) is critically important. For instance, the WTO panel rules on whether member states are complying with the agreed upon rules — rules that facilitate a particular form of trade, called free trade — with other issues being subordinate. The WTO has potentially very wide powers. The following are actions or measures that could be seen to violate the current GATT:

- Measures that restrict imports as a result of a country's more stringent food-safety standards (that country would be forced to either change standards or face sanctions);

- Attempts to control imports on the basis of the process or method of production (for example, rules requiring sustainable production processes and sound labour policies);

- Measures that support locally grown produce or small-scale farmers through subsidies; and

- Rules that regulate the use of genetically engineered organisms in food production (Glassman 1994).

Some leeway is still given in the interpretation and implementation of the Convention on Biological Diversity and the TRIPS agreement. However, environmental and human-rights groups will have to make significant lobbying efforts to steer the discussion toward a more sustainable future.

The current context

Decisions by the US Patent and Trademark Office to grant monopoly rights over plant, animal, and human genetic materials have led to a rush to collect, map, and patent genes, based largely on their future profit potential. Despite the pressure from trade agreements such as GATT, few governments endorse the IPR system accepted by US courts (CS Canada 1996b). Meanwhile, the United States has accused developing countries of engaging in unfair trading practices when they fail to recognize US patents within their own national boundaries. A strong US lobby, for example, aims to force all countries to recognize patents on seeds (Lehman 1994).

The corporate demand for IPR to biodiversity is based on the false premise that only their investments need to be rewarded. The toil of Southern farmers in domesticating, breeding, and conserving biodiversity over centuries is conveniently forgotten. The existing IPR agreements fail to recognize the rights of indigenous and local communities to their own knowledge and innovations. As Shiva (1995b, p. 71) remarked, "There is no epistemological justification for treating some *germplasm* as valueless and common heritage and other germplasm as a valuable commodity and private property. This distinction is not based on the nature of the germplasm, but on the nature of political and economic power." Various concerned groups have

Human biological material

Human genes and cell lines are becoming subject to private ownership. The US Patent and Trademark Office has already issued more than 1 250 patents on human gene sequences. More than 100 human cell lines have been subject to patent applications in the United States (RAFI 1996a), although the very few patents that were approved were later revoked. (Cell lines are cells from living organisms that are sustained and grown indefinitely in an artificial medium.) In 1993, a patent claim was filed on the cell line of a woman from Panama. International protest led to the withdrawal of the patent claim in November 1993. In March 1995, the US government granted one of its agencies exclusive rights to all genetic materials contained in the cell line of a Papua New Guinean man (CS Canada 1996c). This patent was withdrawn in December 1996.

labeled this state of affairs an "exploitive asymmetry," "the West's new frontier," and "biopiracy."

Developing countries have strongly argued that multinationals from the industrialized world exploit their biological wealth and then sell the patented products back to them at excessive prices. With the growth of the biotechnology industries, in combination with the loss of biological diversity worldwide, the access to and control of genetic resources have attracted the attention of governments, corporations, and others — mainly because of the tremendous potential for generating commercial profits. The traditional lifestyles, knowledge, and biogenetic resources of indigenous peoples have become commodities, to be bought, sold, and traded.

TRIPS and the Convention on Biological Diversity have made it clear that IPR law is an important issue for all to consider, and in particular, for indigenous peoples to consider. If corporations can secure IPR protection for their inventions then indigenous peoples, too, should be entitled to protection for their intellectual property.

What does this mean to a rural farmer?

As a rule, farmers save some of their crop to use as seed in the following year. With the US IPR regimes, farmers would have to pay royalties on the seeds from patented seeds — even in the case where farmers were the source of the original stocks, those farmers would not be allowed under GATT to market or use them. The IPR to a folk variety would include the rights to control the use of the folk variety and the rights to the information coded in the DNA as a result of selection by farmers and their farming systems (Soleri and Cleaveland 1993). (Royalties may also have to be paid for patented animals.)

Commercial plant breeding is in the hands of a few TNCs that now control all the significant gene banks. TNCs are developing plants that respond to their own agrochemicals. TNCs are also working on genetic modifications aimed at converting nonhybrid fertile plants, such as wheat, into sterile hybrids. If a gene from another plant could induce sterility, seeds would have to be purchased each year. If IPR systems continue to evolve in the current direction, farmers' prospects include paying royalties for patented seeds; becoming dependent on one supplier for seed, fertilizers, herbicides, and pesticides; and, in the case of hybrid, sterile plants, buying new seeds each year.

Much debate is needed at the international level. A focal question is whether IPR, which were developed to protect industrial inventions, are appropriate for human or other biological genetic materials. And how can

The Human Genome Diversity Project

The Human Genome Diversity Project (HGDP) proposes to draw blood and tissue samples from some 700 indigenous groups, from 722 communities. The mandate of the HGDP is to collect and maintain the genetic samples and manage the database (Harry 1995a). The HGDP does not plan to do genetic engineering but has no safeguards to prevent others from doing so with the collected samples (Harry 1995b). Although some of this genome research could have benevolent applications (DNA from remote populations has been found useful in the development of vaccines), historically, disturbing links appeared between the collection and study of blood and tissue samples from indigenous peoples and military programs of the United States. Before 1972, the US Navy was investigating ways to target the medical vulnerabilities of specific ethnic populations (CS Canada 1996b). The point is that this information could become data for racist purposes.

Once blood and tissue samples are taken, it may prove difficult to have them repatriated. In a landmark 1990 California Supreme Court decision, it was established that a "donor" does not have a "property right" to the tissues removed from his or her body. In this case, the man's cells were used to develop valuable antibacterial and cancer-fighting pharmaceuticals. The Court's ruling made it clear that the donor was not entitled to share in the profits derived from the commercial use of his cells or any other products resulting from research on any of his biological materials (Harry 1995b).

such mechanisms protect a nonphysical entity such as oral IK? Countries do need to decide what type of mechanisms to adopt to protect themselves: IPR systems or other types of mechanisms (for example, common intellectual rights, traditional resource rights). As it is, the cost and administrative implications of adopting some of the new IPR systems are significant: 250 000 USD per patent (RAFI 1996b). At the very least, farmers must retain the absolute right to save seed, to experiment with exotic germplasm, and to exchange seeds (RAFI 1995).

Some IPR issues

On the Convention on Biological Diversity, a number of issues remain outstanding:

- How can a country restrict access to its genetic resources?

- If access is granted, how can traditional IK about genetic resources be protected?

- If access is granted, how can law and policy be used to ensure that a fair share of the benefits from any products derived from genetic resources is returned to local communities?

An IPR approach is unacceptable to many indigenous groups

For indigenous peoples, life is a common property which cannot be owned, commercialized and monopolized by individuals... Accordingly, the patenting of any life forms and processes is unacceptable to indigenous peoples (Sabah, Malaysia, February 24–27, 1995).

We reaffirm that imperialism is perpetuated through intellectual property rights systems, science and modern technology to control and exploit the lands, territories and resources of indigenous peoples (Suva, Fiji, April 1995).

Source: CS Canada (1996a)

If access is granted, one approach to protecting people's genetic resources is to have governments prohibit TNCs from patenting materials found on indigenous peoples' lands.

On many of these complex IPR questions and issues, indigenous peoples from around the globe have made their position clear. The following box presents some of their key statements on those topics, highlighting the fundamental links between IK and indigenous rights to land and resources.

At the community level, researchers cannot detach themselves from such questions. Appropriate arrangements need to be made for in-country recording, storing, application, and transfer of local IK within and between national and international communities. At the local level, the following are relevant questions:

- How can local people be protected from exploitation of their knowledge and resources?

- How are consent and participation defined?

- Who is authorized to give consent? Should consent be required by individuals, the governing body of the local area, or both? Can consent be granted by the nation state on behalf of local people?

- How should local people be compensated for the information they provide?

- How should research projects be designed so that local people benefit?

- How should IK be stored so that local people can access and benefit from it?

Strong indigenous voices on the topics of "benefit sharing," "participation," and "consent"

- "What is equitable will be determined by indigenous peoples themselves" (Julayinbul, Mataatua).

- "No benefit sharing agreement, whether agreed to by individuals and communities or imposed by external forces, can extinguish or reduce the inherent rights of indigenous peoples" (Santa Cruz, Julayinbul, Kari-Oca).

- "Indigenous peoples' rights pertaining to knowledge and biodiversity are collectively held" (Santa Cruz).

- "Participation and consent must necessarily include both indigenous men and indigenous women" (Kari-Oca, Quito, Beijing).

- "The right to consent includes the right to refuse" (Suva, Phoenix, Jakarta, Santa Cruz, Julayinbul, Mataatua, Oka, Pe ang, Amsterdam).

- "Consent cannot be freely granted under conditions of political, economic or social coercion or in the absence of effective mechanisms to protect indigenous peoples' rights" (Jakarta, Mataatua, Phoenix, Beijing).

- "We call a moratorium on the collection of biological material until local and indigenous communities are in a position to assert their rights over their resources and knowledge" (Jakarta 1995).

- "Biological resources taken from indigenous peoples without proper consent must be repatriated" (Suva, Treaty, Phoenix, Beijing, Kari-Oca).

- "Indigenous people have a right to full disclosure about any investigation or use of their knowledge or resources" (Kari-Oca, Tapirisat).

- "We reaffirm that indigenous peoples have the fundamental right to deny access to, refuse to participate in, or allow removal or appropriation by external scientific projects, of any genetic materials" (Phoenix).

- "We declare indigenous peoples are willing to share our knowledge with humanity provided we determine when, where and how it is used. At present the international system does not recognize or respect our past, present and future contributions" (Suva, Fiji, April 1995).

Source: CS Canada (1996d)

Compensation mechanisms

A number of mechanisms, including funds, contracts and IPR agreements, nonbinding agreements, and defensive publications, are used for compensation, benefit sharing, and the protection of IPR. These same mechanisms can be applied to IK. A more comprehensive discussion of these mechanisms can be found in Posey and Dutfield's (1996) book, *Beyond Intellectual Property: Toward Traditional Resource Rights for Indigenous Peoples and Local Communities.*

Funds

- Companies can establish funds to compensate communities for IK that is widely distributed but unattributable because the original innovators are anonymous or no longer living. This type of mechanism can support a wide variety of regional goals, such as biodiversity-conservation programs.

Contracts and IPR agreements

- Contracts — legally binding agreements between two or more parties that enable the contractees to take legal action on their own behalf — may be appropriate if knowledge and resources are not widely known and are not in the public domain. A community's contract with a company may give the community, among other rights, a per-sample fee, advance payments, reports on the research results, local training, royalties on compounds, and the option of filing a joint patent with the company or of having local community members named as inventors. Contracts can address issues of confidentiality and exclusivity. A confidentiality clause can ensure that the knowledge or material will not be made available to anyone else without the community's permission. The company may request exclusive rights to the information or material supplied.

- Material-transfer agreements (MTAs) establish standards for the transfer of biological resources and outline the benefits to the supplier (for example, up-front benefits, a trust fund, or future royalties). When the material has commercial potential, MTAs usually grant the commercial party the right to apply for patents.

- Information-transfer agreements (ITAs) move one step beyond MTAs. ITAs give communities the right to be compensated for material transfer and also to be recognized for their intellectual contribution by having community members named as inventors in the patent application or by being able to file a joint patent with the company.

- Licencing agreements enable a community to sell a patent to a company that is better equipped to commercialize a product. Under a licencing agreement, a company pays fees to the community for knowledge (or samples); the community transfers this particular knowledge only to the company during the period that the licencing agreement is in effect.

Nonbinding agreements

- A letter of intent or a memorandum of understanding is a statement of principles between parties that serves as a framework for a future legally binding contract. A letter of intent or a memorandum of understanding can address issues of confidentiality, the sharing of research results, and the provision of benefits but is not legally enforceable.

- Covenants establish principles for future legally binding agreements and often contain ethical commitments.

Defensive publications

- An inventor may publish a thorough description detailing how to practice the invention; after the date of publication, any patent claim for the same invention will be invalid.

The quantity and form of compensation for IK are complex issues. How much compensation is both just and realistic? Compensation should probably depend on how closely the commercial product is related to the traditional compound or use. If a community contributes knowledge and resources only during the early stages of research, royalties can be as low as 1–5%. If the commercial product is based on an indigenous product, royalties can be as high as 10–15% (Posey and Dutfield 1996). The details of such arrangements will have to be negotiated on a case-by-case basis.

Emerging mechanisms for dealing with IPR

Governments, university researchers, nongovernmental organizations (NGOs), corporations, and others are generating ideas and new approaches and mechanisms to deal with indigenous intellectual property. A few examples are given below to convey the breadth of what are at times conflicting approaches and conflicting paradigms.

A government example

The first Brazilian biodiversity law was passed in the state of Acre in July 1997. The law, a response to biopiracy, makes it compulsory for foreign scientists and companies to associate with a Brazilian group before they can carry out any research activities. The law also requires the foreign parties to leave part of the collected materials in Brazil (Cimi 1997).

A university example

A gene extracted from a rice variety from Mali was patented by the University of California at Davis (UCD). This gene confers resistance to blight and has good potential for being transferred to other rice varieties and to other plants. The potential financial and ecological benefits (avoidance of fungicidal sprays) may be of great value.

The chief inventor initiated a novel mechanism to compensate the source nation. A gene fund was established with a 150 000 USD advance share on royalties. UCD will funnel into this fund 25% of its share of future royalties, reviewing this commitment when its contribution reaches 52 500 USD. The three codiscoverers will contribute an undetermined portion of their royalties. Companies that buy licences to develop products using the gene will contribute some of their future profits. Seed companies, growers, and other corporate gainers will be encouraged to pay a small tax to support conservation efforts.

The fund will provide UCD scholarships to students from Mali, where the rice originated; other West African countries where the landrace grows; and from the Philippines, where the breeding work was done to incorporate the gene into cultivated lines.

This benefit-sharing mechanism is the first of its kind, and its effectiveness in helping rural communities to develop, conserve, and use biodiversity will need to be carefully monitored. For instance, the school dropout rate in high-biodiversity areas is typically high — it will therefore require extra effort to identify suitable candidates and to ensure that scholarships are awarded in targeted regions, rather than to individuals in privileged areas. Once students have received their foreign degrees, mechanisms will need to be in place to ensure that graduates return to their home country — to avoid a brain drain there. Furthermore, sharing royalties with the institute that stores and researches the germplasm (the International Rice Research Institute in the Philippines in this case) may deplete benefits intended for the donor region. Such research institutes could become claimants for every germplasm they store.

Some people debate whether this compensatory package is fair and the amount appropriate (it is impossible to assess the true value of the invention at this time); whether the instrument of benefit sharing (that is, scholarships) will be effective; whether the fund is feasible, given the voluntary nature of some of the private-sector contributions; and whether other mechanisms, such as trust funds that support local conservation efforts, are also needed. However, the inherent limitations have been considered less important than the real need to get compensation programs organized (Gupta 1997).

A researcher's opinion on informing communities about benefits

Fernandez (1994) recommended that researchers clearly outline the purpose of their research and explain how the project will serve the community. For instance, the community should be told whether the IK project will

- Identify resources that can be used for the benefit of the community;

- Identify common problems and develop interventions beneficial to the community;

- Improve IK practices;

- Provide information of importance for commerce or the advancement of science; and

- Provide appropriately designed education materials based on the research output.

The community should be informed about any proposed follow-up activities — for example, marketing, processing for marketing or consumption, planting (nurseries to provide food or medicinal plants or to improve the availability of plant resources), and agroforestry projects. The community should also be informed that its knowledge may be used for conservation, medicine, new drugs, new crops, the timber industry, pest control, nutrition and food processing, or new farming systems, as the case may be.

An NGO's suggestions regarding discoveries

The Four Worlds International Institute for Indigenous Sciences has suggested that, if interesting discoveries are made during the course of an IK research initiative (FWIIIS 1995–96),

- Special brokerage arrangements be negotiated with the original holders of IK to patent and market the discoveries;

- Portions of the database be marketed in a variety of media formats; and

Table1. Protecting intellectual property rights at the community level: a suggested checklist for researchers

The preliminary preparations

- The funding application is prepared in collaboration with any indigenous people living in the area
- Researchers agree in writing to respect the intellectual property rights of local people
- The community management structures are fully involved in developing the research program
- Community representatives help establish guidelines and policies
- The researchers, the community, and each informant sign an agreement before the start of any research activity

The agreement

The agreement between the researcher and the community outlines the following:

- Who "owns" the indigenous knowledge, and who can use it
- Restrictions on the publication of certain types of information (for example, secret rituals)
- How and by whom the information will be collected
- The location of the research activity, including a list of any sacred sites
- Responsibilities of each party
- Adequate compensation for local experts who provide information
- Expected benefits for and impacts on the community and the researchers
- Reporting requirements during the research activity
- The community's role in the review of all final reports of the research
- How the information will be made available to the community, how it will be released to others, and the number of report copies, including photographs and other research products (for example, plant collections), that the community will receive at the conclusion of the activity
- The sponsor's rights over the final report
- Copyright arrangements, including any arrangements for coauthorship of publications

If any information (for example, plant variety or local technology) is commercialized (or has potential to be commercialized), the agreement indicates

- A requirement to negotiate with the original holders of the knowledge any arrangements for how to proceed

Policies

If the research involves the use of cultural artefacts (for example, indigenous songs or cultural symbols) or the removal of biological samples (for example, livestock, fungus, folk varieties), policies should be developed to regulate the following:

- The use of folk variety names and other cultural symbols in connection with the marketing of seeds or food products
- The collection, use, and distribution of biological materials by outsiders
- Restrictions on any commercialization of the collected species

Source: Compiled by author

- A videotape documenting the successful indigenous experiments be produced and marketed to industry, government, human-service agencies, international-development agencies, and educational institutions.

IPR issues add a degree of risk and complexity to the IK research process. Table 1 suggests some protocols. These are a starting point for researchers who aim to protect IPR at the community level. This checklist will need to be revised and updated for a specific context and as IPR issues evolve.

Developing a Research Framework

This section presents some considerations for those who are developing a framework for IK research. IK research has borrowed and benefited from a number of sources and disciplines. Included here are methodological contributions from the International Union for the Conservation of Nature and Natural Resources (IUCN) and from social science research, gender-sensitive research, and participatory rural appraisal research that are relevant to current IK research practice. Other relevant factors, including IPR issues from Section 2, are brought together in Table 3 ("A research-framework summary for IK research") at the end.

IUCN: an approach to assessing progress toward sustainability

According to IUCN (1997), a society is sustainable when the human condition and the condition of the ecosystem are satisfactory or improving. IUCN has developed a series of eight (short) volumes to assess actions in terms of progress toward sustainability.

The materials share four key principles: wholeness, asking questions, reflective institutions, and people focused. *Wholeness* refers to the need to treat people and the environment together, as equally important. Because people–environment interactions are not well understood, the principle of wholeness leads to *asking (good) questions,* before searching for indicators. Asking (good) questions requires the context of *reflective institutions,* where people will question and learn together. The approach will be *people focused* because appropriate actions will influence human behaviour.

The IUCN series includes the following:

- Three methods for system assessment: Participatory and Reflective Analytical Mapping, Assessing Rural Sustainability, and Planning Action for Rural Sustainability;

- One method for organizational assessment: Reflective Institutions; and

- Three tools: Barometer of Sustainability, Community-based Indicators, and Questions of Survival.

In the IUCN framework, progress toward sustainability involves actions founded on a cycle of action-and-reflection: an action is formulated after an initial diagnosis of the situation; the action is monitored during implementation; and after evaluation of the results of the action, the next action is formulated. Each action is considered an experiment and a learning opportunity. The eight volumes of this approach form an integrated whole and are best used as a comprehensive planning tool to guide project planning and actions. (Interested readers should contact IUCN to receive the complete package.) The IUCN approach or some other reflective planning process plus some good questions should guide the research process from the planning stage onward.

Conducting social science research

Much IK research relies on social science techniques and, in particular, interviews that yield qualitative rather than quantitative data. Researchers have a variety of ideas for designing and conducting a good interview. The following subsections offer some tips and generalizations to help researchers with the selection of community researchers, the setting for interviews, the phrasing of interview questions, and the choice of group or individual interviews. The common sources of error associated with interview data are also listed.

IK researchers are often "outsiders" (for example, urban professionals or foreigners) working across cultures. Cross-cultural considerations are paramount and should influence the interview design, so researchers will need to review and adapt these tips to the specific cultural context of their own research.

The interview process

Community researchers
Selecting appropriate community researchers is critical to the success of any study. Although a high level of education and literacy better enables interviewers to grasp the complexity of some of the (survey) questions and to aid in any transcription process, motivation and enthusiasm are key to the

> Community researchers will help ensure that the interview questions are well designed and suitable.

success of the interviewers (Barker and Cross 1992). The community researchers should also have a high level of curiosity and analytical capacity; an understanding of their own culture and how research among their own people should be conducted; a good traditional education; and the confidence and respect of the villagers (von Geusau et al. 1992).

The setting

Interviews are best conducted in a place where the informant is most comfortable, usually in a familiar setting relevant to the topic (for example, in a garden if the interview topic is gardening). If IK interviews are conducted in a setting removed from the topic, some informants may have difficulty remembering, describing, or discussing the subject in detail. For instance, without specimen samples, an informant may be unable to distinguish between various species — something easily done in the field (Johnson 1992).

Interview questions

A question–answer format is not always appropriate. In a study on the learning of indigenous crafts, Kater (1993) found that people were not fully conscious of their learning processes. They never discussed learning processes among themselves and hence found it difficult to be interviewed on a topic they never verbalized. Interviewees failed to understand the researcher's questions. Kater concluded that under those circumstances (where the research topic touches on matters not normally verbalized), interviews could not yield satisfactory results and observation was more important. Kater noted, however, that observation captures one moment in time, only a brief moment in the whole apprenticeship period in this case, and concluded that in this instance, real insight could only be obtained from prolonged observation.

On topics amenable to a question–answer format, it seems to work well to ask specific questions after receiving a full narrative from the respondent (Tester, personal communication, 1997, see p. 6). Questions produce more information when they are split into various components. For example, "Which plants are used for the treatment of cattle or poultry?" will produce more information than "Which plants are used for the treatment of farm animals?" "Which plants are used as fruits or vegetables?" will yield more than "Which plants are food items?" Although both types of question will produce answers, the more specific questions will provide more information (Maundu 1995).

Group interviews

A group that is well briefed on the purpose of the research will be more willing to participate in an interview. The quality and quantity of the information generated by a group over a given period of time will be affected by such factors as size; group composition and psychological state; and social, economic, and cultural factors.

The group should be neither too small nor too large. A very small group (less than 5) may not provide the results expected of a group. A group with more than 40 participants tends to become unmanageable, and many of the participants get no opportunity to express their views. In his experience, Tester (personal communication, 1997, see p. 6) found that 8–12 participants make an ideal group size.

The group's gender and age ratios determine the level of participation of individuals. In mixed groups, men tend to dominate the discussion. Women often feel most comfortable among other women, and in some communities, women (especially younger women) keep quiet in the presence of men. In the absence of women, men are often impatient and irritable. The middle-aged group usually commands more attention than the very young and the very old, and the young often feel shy and inexperienced. In areas with more than one ethnic group, one group may dominate the other. To encourage spontaneity and to minimize inhibitions caused by codes of expected behaviour, the researcher should identify discussion groups on the basis of gender, age, educational status, interests, and ethnicity (Oduol 1996).

Various factors influence the psychological state of the group. The amount of time available will determine whether the group is prepared to provide information. As a rule, women and children have to go home early to do their chores (Maundu 1995).

Group versus individual interviews

Group interviews have both advantages and disadvantages. The accuracy of the information and the rate at which it is generated are higher in groups. One or more members of the group will highlight any uncertainty about the information, and the exercise will identify the more knowledgeable members. Less knowledgeable participants will learn something new. The group interview is particularly useful if time is limited, a list of items needs to be generated, or an issue needs to be clarified. The disadvantages are that vocal people, people in positions of authority (for example, administrators, politicians), and men tend to dominate the discussion; knowledgeable individuals — women, the elderly, and people who are young or shy — may not participate fully, so some of the desired information may be withheld.

Errors and their sources

Social science research techniques (especially surveys and questionnaires) can commingle errors associated with the actual instrument (for example, inappropriate or ambiguous questions), with the interview process (for example, for whatever reason, the respondent cannot or will not answer a question correctly), and with data analysis (for example, data are misinterpreted by the researcher). Designing appropriate interview questions, ensuring a culturally sensitive research process, and crosschecking the information during the research process and data analysis can reduce these errors. Stone and Campbell (1984, cited in Wickham 1993) categorized errors as follows: nonsampling errors; sampling errors; sociocultural errors; courtesy-bias errors; and language and translation errors.

Nonsampling errors caused by the respondent include problems of recall, misunderstood questions, topics too sensitive to discuss with an outsider, and lying. Those caused by the interviewer include recording errors and misinterpretations of the information. Nonsampling errors are generally considered greater than sampling errors.

Sampling errors are associated with generalizations made about a target population based on a sample.

Sociocultural errors emerge when the respondent finds the survey format unfamiliar, uncomfortable, embarrassing, culturally inappropriate, or confusing.

Courtesy-bias errors arise when respondents feel compelled to express only views they think the interviewer wants to hear.

Language and translation errors are associated with the forward translation and back translation of interview questions and interview data. First, the survey words, concepts, and categories can be too technical and unfamiliar for translation into the local language. To reduce this type of error, the survey terms should be made compatible with local ones.

Second, some information is lost during back translation when outside terminology (for example, scientific terms) fail to reflect the indigenous concepts, terms, and categories or fail to capture the subtleties expressed in the indigenous languages. Last, the data are often

> On the issue of matching up IK terms and concepts with those of external knowledge systems, the International Institute of Rural Reconstruction (IIRR) reminds us that local definitions can be broader or narrower than their equivalent. For instance, the local name of one disease may refer to several diseases; local descriptions can be more detailed; one plant may have several names, each describing a stage of growth or an intended use. Other concepts, such as various beliefs, may have no Western equivalent.
>
> *Source: IIRR (1996)*

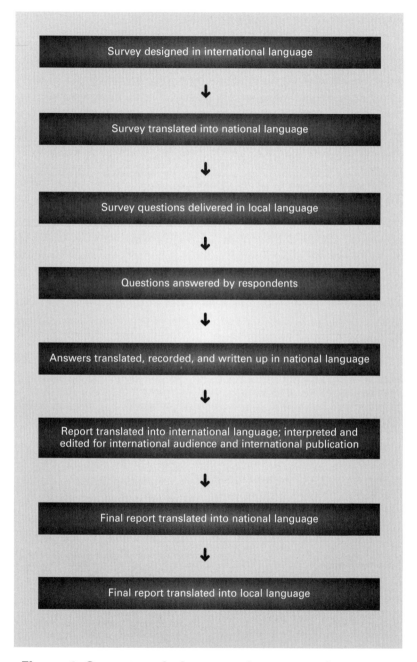

Figure 1. Some translation steps in a research process.
Note: Each step can introduce error. Accurate translation is needed
throughout the research process.

processed through a number of translation steps (Figure 1), at each of which there is the potential to lose some information or to introduce errors.

Translation issues can surface at all levels of a research process, not only for the outside researcher, but even for the community researcher who has fluency in the local language. Ideas and images, particularly old proverbs and sayings, are difficult to translate correctly.

For instance, in the Dene culture, much knowledge is transmitted in the form of stories and legends with metaphors and sophisticated terminology. One young community researcher commented that the elders used "hidden." Not being completely fluent, this researcher was unable to fully translate the concepts expressed by the informant in that older form of the language (Johnson 1992). A similar challenge was encountered by a local researcher from Africa. An old woman told the researcher, "If you want to get rid of a mouse, you have to get rid of the smell of *soubala.*" *Soubala* is a fragrant spice that attracts mice. Initially, the local researcher was unable to translate the idea from Bobo, the local language, into French. The image was new to her. After some prodding, the old woman explained that children were well educated in the past, but not so well educated now. She further explained that this wasn't the children's fault; this generation of mothers was not properly educating the children. "If you want to get rid of a mouse, you have to get rid of the smell of *soubala*" could be translated as "rather than accusing the children because they are poorly educated, accuse the mothers" (Barker and Cross 1992).

Mwesigye (1996) emphasized that poor translation (both forward and back translation) can create an "artificial knowledge conflict" and that scientific knowledge tends to prevail and to dominate in such cases because it is backed by more powerful political, social, cultural, and economic structures. Using an example from a field site in Uganda, he demonstrated that even a concept such as environment required a clear lingualcultural interpretation in the local people's language to ensure that insiders and outsiders were addressing the same topic.

Before conducting IK research, researchers should spend a lot of time deciphering the meaning of local terms and concepts and matching (as closely as possible) the terms with relevant external terminology.

Making research gender sensitive

The word *gender* refers to our identity as women and men — to the characteristics, roles, and values that specific cultures consider feminine or masculine. Growing children learn these characteristics, roles, and values, and social institutions reinforce them (Durno and Chanyapate 1995). Gender relations are lodged in economic and political structures, as well as in everyday life. Because societies determine their own values and gender roles, these roles change over time. From a development perspective, gender should be considered in research and development planning to improve the status of women.

Many development interventions involve technology transfer. Technology and technology transfer are not gender neutral. In many cases, development interventions have had negative impacts on women (for example, increased workload or less control over a resource). Any assessment of technology must therefore consider its gender impact.

Another important reason to focus on gender is that knowledge differs from individual to individual, and gender accounts for a lot of those differences (other factors, such as kinship, age, ethnicity, religious affiliation, and wealth, also contribute to the differentiation of individual knowledge.) Women and men are socialized differently and often function in different spheres of the community. Women and men often know different things. They also possess different knowledge about similar things, use different communication channels to transfer information, and have different interests and needs. The instruction of children often takes place along gender lines (Simpson 1994).

> In the South Pacific, men generally possess the most detailed knowledge of the marine environment, but women have excellent knowledge of the near-shore zone and its fauna of shellfish and crustaceans. The uphill primary rain forest is generally the domain of men, whereas the low-hill garden areas are largely the charge of women.
>
> *Source: Baines and Hviding (1992)*

Of great significance is the fact that work (generally) is organized along gender lines. Women's and men's knowledge reflect their labour responsibilities. Concerning matters of the living environment, women are often the daily managers. Caring for livestock, cultivating specific food and cash crops, collecting wild fruits and leaves, processing, preparing, and preserving food, selecting seeds, and propagating plants are activities assigned to different age and gender groups (Simpson 1994). For instance, a case study of the ethnoveterinary knowledge of Afghan nomads reported that women indeed knew more than men about milking and caring for sick and newborn animals and meat processing because that's what they do (Davis 1995).

Until recently, women's IK systems were considered inferior to men's or regarded as nonknowledge. The knowledge of women as users and innovators of technology was largely dismissed because of the domestic nature of women's work and the fact that women's technology tends to be less prestigious software (techniques and processes of production), rather than hardware (tools and equipment).

Men cannot voice the knowledge of women, and neither men nor women alone can fully represent the knowledge of their community. Together, men and women form a knowledge system specific to local conditions and priorities (Appleton and Hill 1995).

Research aimed at engaging local knowledge systems must capture the different sets of knowledge and pay particular attention to whose knowledge is being included. The inclusion or exclusion of different sets of knowledge will determine to a large extent who benefits. Researchers need to pay greater attention to listening to and learning from men's and women's different experiences, needs, and knowledge.

Gender-sensitive research focuses attention on the research process. Women generally have many roles, and a research activity may interfere with women's daily routines. To ensure that women can participate, the researcher

Women in general

- Are excluded from the processes of problem analysis, planning, and decision-making;

- Have fewer rights than men in marriage, divorce, property ownership, and inheritance;

- Must adhere to community laws decided on by men;

- Own less than 1% of the world's property;

- Have more difficulty obtaining credit because they usually lack collateral (for example, certificates of land ownership);

- Have a lower status in family and community life;

- Are 67% of the world's illiterates (priority is often given to boys' education);

- Receive less food or lower quality food and less health care;

- Constitute the majority of the world's subsistence farmers, producing 50–60% of Asia's food;

- Work for 67% of the world's working hours;

- Earn 10% of the world's income;

- Usually occupy lower status, labour-intensive, lower prestige jobs and engage in nearly all of the nonpaid domestic activities (Simpson 1994);

- Are generally paid less for work of equal value; and

- Are not recognized for the work they do. (For example, when extension training is provided to men on an aspect of the farming system that is usually managed by women, there may be low adoption of the technology, or the men may take over the activity while the women lose their traditional role or income-earning opportunity.)

Source: Durno and Chanyapate (1995)

should consult the women to find out when, where, and how to schedule research activities and who should conduct the interviews. It is the researcher's responsibility to design a process that enables the real participation of women. The researcher must also ensure that if women give information in confidence, their confidentiality is upheld and that the information is reported back to women (in the past, some researchers have collected data from women and then reported the information to men).

In gender-sensitive research, the researcher usually separates all statistics and information by gender (and often age). Disaggregating the information helps to highlight any differences between men and women in terms of roles, needs, and access to and control over resources. Gender analysis is needed to understand the different responsibilities and degrees of power that different actors have in every social situation.

Where

Interviewing women can demand a higher investment of both time and energy: "women are harder to pin down," meaning that it is more difficult for them to postpone their chores. Women often prefer to be interviewed in their homes. In some regions, it is socially unacceptable for women to be seen chatting in public places, and a home setting enables women to continue their chores — looking after the children, guarding the stove, or making crafts. Conversely, in a study set in Nepal, Hinton (1995) found that women preferred to be interviewed in a more public forum, away from home, so that childcare could be delegated to other family members.

How

The researcher must ask women whether they would feel more comfortable with a female interviewer and whether they would prefer to be interviewed singly, in groups of women, or in mixed groups. In some cases, women may be more comfortable in a mixed interview (for example, a husband and wife team); in other cases, men may tend to speak for women or laugh at how women answer questions.

Who

Employing women interviewers can be more difficult than employing men. This difficulty can be associated with cultural constraints restricting the freedom of women to travel. In addition, female interviewers generally have less (formal) work experience than men and generally need more training and confidence building. Barker and Cross (1992) found that once women were trained, they could interview men with ease. In contrast, it was difficult for men to interview women. The male interviewers did not know what to ask the female interviewees, and their interviews quickly broke down.

Finally, it should be noted that marked differences can appear even within villages. Variations in women's roles and status and in men's roles and status, even within a well-defined geographical area, make generalizing along gender lines a delicate activity.

Participatory rural appraisal

In the recent past, rural development planners often did their work without community consultation. When they included consultation, they used quantitative surveys and did not communicate the results back to the people who had shared their knowledge. The consequences were often impractical, ineffective, and culturally unacceptable management decisions. Furthermore, extensive survey research often took a long time.

> "The development profession suffers from an entrenched superiority complex with respect to the small farmer. We believe our modern technology is infinitely superior to his. We conduct our research and assistance efforts as if we knew everything and our clients nothing."
>
> *Source: Hatch (1976), cited in Wickham (1993, p. 30)*

Rapid and participatory research approaches were developed to overcome these limitations.

Rapid rural appraisal (RRA) enables outsiders to understand rural conditions quickly and combines methods from various disciplines to yield relevant data. The key principles guiding RRA investigations are

- *Progressive learning* — With RRA, researchers make no attempt to know all the questions ahead of time, which allows for program changes as learning accumulates;

- *Rapid learning* — Researchers use triangulation (crosschecking data by multiple methods) to quickly validate or refute findings; and

- *Multidisciplinary learning* — A range of disciplines, local informants, and knowledge are brought together (Grandstaff and Grandstaff 1987, cited in Wickham 1993).

Building on RRA, participatory rural appraisal (PRA) employs techniques for learning about rural life and conditions from, with, and by rural people. PRA supports the direct participation of communities, with rural people themselves becoming the main investigators and analysts. Rural people set the priorities; determine research needs; select and train community researchers; collect, document, and analyze data; and plan and implement solutions based on their findings. Actions stemming from this research serve the local community. Outsiders facilitate but do not direct the process (Chambers 1992, cited in Wickham 1993).

PRA is a "people-centred" development model in the tradition of human ecology. A people-centred model focuses on "processes whereby individuals and societies build their capacity to meet their own needs and improve the quality of their own lives" (Durning 1989, cited in Wickham 1993, p.17). Human ecology is the study of the relationships between the natural and human worlds, where cultural beliefs and values often regulate human behaviour and actions. Human ecology borrows the emic and etic perspectives from the field of ethnology. The emic perspective is concerned with how phenomena are perceived and interpreted within a culture. The etic perspective is concerned with the scientific classification and analysis of the role of belief systems in human–environment interactions (Lovelace 1984, cited in Wickham 1993).

PRA places more emphasis than RRA on the following three key principles:

- *Correct behaviour and attitudes* — The PRA researcher must be flexible, creative, patient, respectful, and willing to listen to and be taught by rural people.

- *Multiple methods* — The use of numerous research techniques enables rural people to investigate, analyze, and present their knowledge using familiar terms and materials, and the researcher gains a more complete understanding of people's knowledge.

- *Visually shared information and ideas* — The data are transferred to visual forms (maps, charts, models, graphs) for people to view, discuss, and manipulate. This facilitates mutual learning and helps the researcher crosscheck the information.

The main advantages of PRA are that it

- *Increases participation* — PRA invites rich and poor, illiterate and literate, and powerful and disenfranchised men, women, and children to participate and share their knowledge.

- *Supports independence* — By involving local people from the beginning of the research process, PRA encourages people to determine their own needs.

- *Builds dignity and generates knowledge* — When local people teach, explain, analyze their own knowledge, and plan their own futures, everyone learns and self-esteem increases.

- *Is practical and creative* — PRA's flexible character supports people's inventiveness and creativity (Wickham 1993).

PRA emerged from RRA to reduce the extractive nature of RRA and to enable rural people to create change based on their findings, rather than on outsiders' recommendations. PRA follows no rigid formulae. Practitioners must experiment with, invent, test, adopt, and adapt new methods and techniques to improve and strengthen PRA.

Weaknesses in PRA methodology

As previously mentioned, PRA methodology and PRA techniques have many strengths. This subsection highlights some of its weaknesses. An extensive literature on the limitations associated with PRA techniques is available, and the reader is directed to Mosse (1994) and IIED (1995) for a more comprehensive discussion. Some of the important debates are about power, group processes, and gender; training and techniques; commitment; and expectations. These are summarized below.

Power, group processes, and gender

PRA takes place within local power structures. Power relationships are most visible during group exercises. Villagers are often guided through a structured set of group interviews, with the intent of having villagers articulate and record their knowledge and identify their priorities for intervention. Mosse (1994) labeled these group techniques "public" social events. The public nature of these exercises can create and exclude particular knowledge, as the output is strongly influenced by existing social relations, particularly power, authority, and gender relations. The interviewees are more likely to project the view of the most powerful, especially to create consensus, with the interests of the powerful identified as the common interest. Nondominant people — the poorest people, the women, the children, the minority groups — lack the ability to make public their private opinions and interests. Gender relations, for instance, are heightened in the public setting. Participation of women in group events is usually limited and discontinuous as a result of numerous factors, including women's general exclusion from public spaces and activities.

When power relations within a community are not apparent to outside researchers, PRA-based interventions may increase power and wealth inequities. When group techniques are applied in the early stages of a project to set project objectives and priorities — when the project team may not have a good grasp of the political and social context and where the influence of power and gender inequality are likely to be great — the project's purpose may be significantly compromised. Some researchers suggest that organized PRAs may be appropriate only after a long period of working informally with individuals or neighbourhood groups and that public decision-making be avoided until project workers are familiar with the setting and have built (genuine) good rapport.

To decrease power-related data distortions, researchers can compare and contrast the results of public and household data and monitor participation in the events — not only who is present and who is absent, but also degree of involvement and whose opinions are being presented. Fieldworkers need to be trained in observation and social-analysis skills to observe, analyze, and record the interactions.

Training and techniques

The fast, broad adoption of PRA has created some problems: inadequate training capacity; insufficient training; and routinized application of visual, group, and participatory techniques. Also, the menu of available techniques is incomplete, and researchers using PRA may need to develop additional tools.

The use of participatory methods does not guarantee participation and empowerment. Although learning to use standard PRA techniques may be considered easy, acquiring the facilitation and communication skills to apply them is a challenge. Partly because of the hurry-scurry manner in which PRA has been adopted by intervenors (from small village-level NGOs to World Bank personnel), there has been no quality assurance in terms of PRA trainers and PRA training. Short training-the-trainer courses have proliferated, meaning that some trainers and some fieldworkers enter the field with very little experience.

Fieldworkers may need training in mediation, negotiation, observation, social analysis, process documentation, and reflexivity. Some of this training could enhance the results of PRA exercises by making investigators more critical of their own personal biases, data output, and project actions.

Although visual methods have some documented advantages over other methods, they need to be scrutinized. Visual data may have cultural nuances; drawings can have cryptic meanings. One cannot guarantee that participants won't see things differently or have varying visual literacy skills; or that investigators will interpret the maps and drawings in the same way. Visual tools may also have a gender bias. Some aspects of women's experience may not be amenable to those formats. Women may have their own preferred ways of communicating, such as through singing. Maps, tables, matrix rankings, and charts may be more familiar or applicable to men; or they may be viewed by all participants as foreign — it may be more effective to use and adapt local games.

Group methods are often favoured because of their perceived efficiency and problem-solving potential, but as mentioned under "Power, group processes, and gender," these methods bring complex social processes and gender inequities into play. Researchers using group techniques may also make some questionable assumptions — for instance, that groups of women will be available at central locations away from work sites for large blocks of time. Depending on the context, some short-duration, neighbourhood-based activities in nonpublic settings, where simple techniques (informal interviewing) are used, can yield data that complement or challenge group data.

PRA is not the "only way." A number of field reports indicate that some nonparticipatory methods (for example, social-analysis techniques or techniques to assess the impact of participatory work), used in conjunction with participatory techniques, can yield very useful data. Some researchers advise that PRA techniques are best used after the investigator has an intimate knowledge of the area; nonparticipatory techniques (RRA tools or conventional research) can get the investigator to that position more quickly.

Those using PRA methodology need to develop and test additional techniques; the training curriculum should also be expanded. PRA offers no techniques for exploring social complexity or for dealing with the conflicts that PRA may expose or provoke. Some critics debate whether PRA methods can capture nonlinguistic knowledge — for example, knowledge used in making instant judgments that comes from extensive experience and practice. It may be that this knowledge can only be learned by observation and practice. The big challenge is to use and generate methods that will better serve the needs of participatory planning.

Commitment

PRA may require long-term commitments from researchers. Because of the pressures of short-term funding and a demand for quick results, PRA exercises are often generated in one-off 3- to 5-day sessions or short-term assignments. Unfortunately, what happens after these short interventions is, for the most part, unreported. Long-term practitioners have sharply criticized the jet-set consultancy practice and argue that expectations for rapid achievements should be reduced. They argue that intensive, long-term field research, with continuous coaching and interaction, is more effective.

Expectations

The information generated in PRA exercises is shaped by the participants' and the investigator's expectations. What participants choose to share will be influenced by what people think the purpose of the PRA exercise is, who is present and takes part, where it takes place, what people perceive the potential outcome to be, and whether people feel that what they are doing is useful or has some purpose. The information generated in PRAs is shaped by the investigator's presence, interests, and enthusiasm for a particular topic and by what the investigator chooses to record as knowledge. The knowledge produced is also influenced by the specific techniques chosen and by the style of interaction with community members (Mosse 1994; IIED 1995).

A research activity can raise the expectations of community members, which may bring undesirable political consequences from internal and external sources. Care must be taken to ensure that community members' expectations remain realistic.

Finally, outside researchers have to recognize that through their interactions with the community, their own activity contributes to cultural transformation.

Approaches for IK research

IK research presents a list of generic and specific challenges. Together, these challenges call for researchers to be a little more humble, patient, determined, sensitive, flexible, creative, unconventional, open minded, critical, and cautious. A commitment to positive social change and to conducting "enriching", (also called enhancing) research is needed. ("Extractive research" provides information to outsiders, whereas "enriching research" benefits local communities [IIRR 1996]).

> "The experts are the people who have lived a traditional life, not the people who collect traditional knowledge information."
>
> *Source: Unknown*

Research challenges include the following:

- Knowledge is power, so individuals are not always willing to share knowledge among themselves, or with outsiders. Knowledge is a source of status and income (as is the case, for example, with a herbalist) and is often jealously guarded. A related issue is that some indigenous peoples fear that their IK will be misused, and lacking the power to prevent such abuses, they choose to keep quiet (Doubleday 1993).

Mwinyimbegu (1996) further cautioned against the unregulated transfer of IK from the South to the North — theft, really. The quality and quantity of information resulting from a particular research activity depend on the trust established between the researchers and the participants.

In Thailand, von Geusau et al. (1992) found that interviewees disliked answering questions about their personal or economic affairs unless they believed that by doing so, their life would improve.

- IK is considered parochial, confined to a small area, and limited to what rural people can sense, observe, and comprehend using their own terms and concepts. Care must be taken when the intent is to transfer the information to other locations: it may not be applicable elsewhere.

- IK is not uniformly spread. Individuals vary in their aptitude for learning, storing, and generating knowledge. Specialized knowledge often belongs to certain groups or individuals (for example, male elders, midwives, traditional healers). A good sampling strategy or an effective way to identify knowledgeable individuals is needed. It may also be difficult to differentiate traditional knowledge from random local views (Eythorsson 1993). The researcher should use multiple methods to crosscheck the collected data.

- IK includes both explicit and implicit knowledge, some of it intuitively practiced through cultural rituals or revealed through stories and legends. Local knowledge may not be apparent to outsiders or explicitly articulated by local residents, making it difficult for outsiders to understand, record, interpret, or apply.

- IK is embedded in culture (see "Cultural boundaries" box).

- IK systems can be complex. For instance, maintaining biodiversity at the farm level includes maintaining the different varieties and the management processes these varieties are subject to (Loevinsohn and Sperling 1995). Attempts to "scientize" IK by removing it from its owners will tend to compromise the subtle nuances of this knowledge (Thrupp 1989, cited in Wickham 1993).

- IK is more than science. If science is just a small part of knowledge, treating IK as science diminishes its breadth and value. Science and IK intersect in certain subject areas, such as technology, resource

Incorporating local knowledge into development action

In a village in northern Pakistan, government departments provided water and sanitation services, promoting pour-flush latrines and water pipes. These solutions malfunctioned as a result of technical problems (freezing water) and social resistance. The Aga Khan Health Service NGO wanted to develop appropriate local alternatives that reflected the views and preferences of the population. Participatory and sustainable methods of implementation were endorsed. Initially, the research team had to adjust to their new role as facilitators, focused on studying the knowledge, preferences, and problems of local men and women (instead of their usual role as experts and providers of solutions and services). Both villagers and employees of other organizations occasionally criticized the project staff for not building "visible structures" and, hence, for wasting money. Most of the criticism ceased after the first year, once successful trials were implemented.

It took 2 years to complete the fieldwork, translate knowledge into plans, carry out tests, and get the plans accepted by the stakeholders. Time-consuming activities included reporting and documenting the project activities; translating IK into appropriate plans (many internal meetings); convincing outsiders of the quality of the recommendations and the need to implement them (many external meetings); and conducting practical and visible experiments in the field. The first-year studies concentrated on rapid assessments through interviews, group discussions with villagers, village walks, and observation. Based on these findings, the NGO selected the topics for in-depth study. These subsequent studies made use of group discussions, structured observations, PRA tools (drawing, mapping), and surveys (including knowledge, attitude, and practice surveys).

Translating knowledge into action

Preliminary investigations had revealed that compost latrines were very common in one area. For farmers, the contents of the latrines were indispensable field manure. The participants and the project team decided that it was better to incorporate this type of latrine into the plans than to promote the pour-flush latrine. Initially, government employees and other NGOs were less accepting of the plans because they considered improved compost latrines and traditional water pits as being old-fashioned compared with the modern pour-flush latrine. Nevertheless, the project engineers focused on the technical components of these latrines; the social scientists interviewed people about their use patterns and management practices; and the microbiologists checked the pathogen level inside the latrines and in the manure on the fields. After some discussions with all concerned, the engineers developed a safer version of the existing latrine. Trial latrines were constructed for six families and tested for 2 years, with good results. Other villagers now want to construct similar latrines.

Source: Langendijk (1996)

management, ecology, and the classification of living organisms (Emery 1997).

- IK research can foster local empowerment. Host governments may view local empowerment as a subversive challenge to existing political structures (Thrupp 1989, cited in Wickham 1993).

Western science and IK

Many of the challenges of IK research relate directly or indirectly to the difficulty of studying a subordinate knowledge system (that is, IK) using the dominant knowledge system (that is, Western science). The two knowledge systems may in fact be closer than the dichotomy implies. Similarities appear across the two categories, and differences appear within

> "Knowledge is too vast and exalted a subject to be compartmentalised into watertight chambers with names like 'indigenous' or 'scientific'. Nor are the terms indigenous and scientific mutually exclusive."
>
> Source: Jain and Lahta (1996)

them. Agrawal (1996) stated that the critical difference between IK and scientific knowledge lies in their relationship to power and that it is not the holders of IK who exercise the power to marginalize.

Some academics and many indigenous peoples do not find it useful to separate IK from international science. However, IK typically gains legitimacy only when it conforms to

> The Dene people from northern Canada want their knowledge to be referred to as "Dene science"!

the theory and practice of Western knowledge. Even when scientists and bureaucrats promote IK, they usually use scientific categories and methods to collect, verify, and validate it (Johnson 1992). A related problem is that the scientific community prefers to deal with quantitative data, rather than with the interview or qualitative data that characterize IK, IK research, and some of the social sciences (Sallenave 1994).

In general, the following issues define the current context of IK research in a world where Western science sets the rules:

- IK lacks legitimacy and is perceived as being outside conventional scientific understanding. Many environmental scientists regard traditional knowledge as anecdotal, nonquantitative, out of date, and amethodological; others argue that it lacks scientific rigour and objectivity. Related to this point is how the holders of traditional knowledge view their own knowledge. Some local people may view their own knowledge as "backward."

> Barker and Cross (1992) found that many rural inhabitants were reluctant to explain their methods of animal treatment, land conservation, or herbal medicine for fear of being labeled "ignorant" or "out of touch" with the modern world. Once Barker and Cross began to talk in positive terms about traditional techniques from other areas, informants began to share their own knowledge.

Cultural boundaries

Views on the practical application of traditional knowledge can be extremely polarized and uncritical at both ends. Laghi (1997) recounts an interesting story in *The Globe and Mail,* Canada's national newspaper. Four years earlier, the government of the Northwest Territories in northern Canada had adopted IK as official policy. This policy states that traditional knowledge must be incorporated into government actions where appropriate, including decisions about siting diamond mines and setting hunting quotas. The civil service, industry, and legal experts were uncertain about how the policy should be applied. Some wanted its use scaled back, In November 1996, a senior policy adviser with the territorial government and her husband provoked an acrimonious debate with an article on traditional knowledge and environmental assessment. In brief, the couple stated that the government had not defined how the spiritual component of IK (especially materials that refer to a Creator) could be used to formulate public policy, accused the government of imposing native spirituality on the Canadian public, and argued that it is not the role of the public service to promote native spiritualism. They suggested that because traditional knowledge can be anything that traditional knowledge holders say it is, it can be used to justify any enterprise, including the over-exploitation of resources. To illustrate their claim, they recounted the story of three Inuit hunters who violated a ban on killing bowhead whales so as to give an elder his last taste of the delicacy. In traditional lore, the whale presented itself to the hunters to be killed because it knew the desires of the elder.

Bureaucrats, politicians, and native leaders were outraged by the article. The senior policy adviser was suspended from her job, and her government contract was not renewed. The couple was labeled disrespectful, naive, and mischievous for portraying traditional knowledge as unworthy of serious consideration. This story masks layers of issues, both contemporary and historical. It conceals some cultural boundaries. It may be that a spiritual perspective is a more valid way to see and function within our world. The story also reflects the historical power imbalances between Aboriginal groups and their white colonizers, and it reflects the social damage caused by the imposition of (racist) government policies. It shows Aboriginal peoples' continuing mistrust of government policymakers and of an outside knowledge system that abused them in the past. The story also illustrates some government actors' continuing disrespect for Aboriginal people (Whelan, personal communication, 1997).[2]

As history will attest, all types of knowledge — including indigenous and scientific — can be misused by insiders and outsiders. With respect to this particular story, the cultural distance between the bureaucrats who completely opposed having IK enter into decision-making processes and some Aboriginal groups that fervently refused to have their knowledge systems subjected to any form of verification seems unfathomable. A middle ground is needed for critical minds to scrutinize and evaluate the merits and usefulness of knowledge. According to Satterthwaite (1997), this middle ground can be philosophically defined, in part, as the cultural transformation that occurs when traditional knowledge is evaluated from the perspective of the three spheres of knowledge: the objective (the true), the intersubjective (the good — the moral or political), and the personal (the beautiful — the expressive or aesthetic), which allows different people to come to some understanding across cultural boundaries.

Indigenous peoples have demonstrated through their own use and application of IK and their own survival that their knowledge systems are based on sound concepts. There is now mounting scientific evidence that IK concepts are sound, and these concepts should be able to stand up to assessment and evaluation. This will require a stronger commitment to understanding knowledge across cultures.

---

[2] I.M. Whelan, Program Director, Cultural Survival Canada, Ottawa, ON, Canada, personal communication, 1997.

- Professional biases continue to give credence to formally trained personnel, rather than to local experts (Thrupp 1989, cited in Wickham 1993).

- International science is "reductionist," meaning that systems can be understood in terms of their isolated parts. It categorizes specialities according to a hierarchy, manages these components separately, and separates the natural and the physical world from the human world. In the Western scientific system, agriculture is distinct from forestry; the management of wildlife resources becomes separate from the management of the lands and waters that sustain them; and managers become distinct from harvesters. IK emphasizes a holistic approach. Holism is based on the view that systems are more than the sum of their parts. Shifting cultivation is a livelihood strategy that integrates agriculture and forestry; local people are involved with management and harvesting. Indigenous cultures often perceive humans and nature as linked; a Creator is viewed by many cultures as being responsible for ensuring that overall order is maintained in the system. (To repeat two earlier points, IK is more than science; IK is embedded in culture.)

> The indigenous people from Old Crow, Yukon, Canada, have stated, "All too often we read that traditional knowledge must be integrated into conventional scientific methods. The people of Old Crow say that scientific methods and conventional systems of resource management must learn to fit into their traditional ways of viewing and using the land, for these values form the basis for their future survival."
>
> *Source: MacPherson and Netro (1989, p. 25)*

- Results of participatory IK-based projects are incremental and qualitative in nature, which makes it difficult to measure success if success needs to be measured using the type of quantitative indicators preferred by most development agencies (Thrupp 1989, cited in Wickham 1993).

Western science is changing. All of its precepts have been challenged, including its rationalism, objectivism, reductionism, and positivism (which affirms that only the empirically observable or verifiable is scientifically real). Many academics and development workers are trying to introduce holistic concepts to accommodate the interconnectiveness of biological, psychological, and social phenomena (Johnson 1992). But at this time, it can be argued that taking a scientific approach to the study of IK is insufficient. International scientific methods (alone) are too simple to capture the complexity of an IK system. IK research must capture both the tangible and the invisible (see Table 2).

Despite the long list of methodological challenges for IK research, very little attention has been given to the specific requirements of IK research.

Table 2. Common distinctions made between international science and IK.

Area of comparison	IK	International science
Relationship	Subordinate	Dominant
Dominant mode of thinking	Intuitive Holistic	Analytical Reductionist
	Mind and matter considered together	Mind reduced to matter
Communication	Oral, storytelling, singing, dance	Literate
	Subjective	Objective
Instruction	Learned through observation or hands-on experience	Got taught and learned in a situation usually separated from the applied context
Effectiveness	Slow Inconclusive	Fast Conclusive
Data creation	Based on personal observations, trial and error, and synthesis of facts	Based on experimentation and systematic, deliberate accumulation of facts
	Data generated by resource users	Data generated by a specialized cadre of researchers
Data type	Qualitative	Quantitative
	Historical (long time-series one locality)	Statistical (short time-series over a large area)
Explanation	Spiritual Moral	Hypothesis, laws Mechanistic Value free
Classification	Ecological	Generic and hierarchical

Source: Wolfe et al. (1992) and Berkes (1993).

Whelan (personal communication, 1997, see p. 50) captures the core values associated with doing IK research in terms of 3 *R*s: respect, reciprocity, and relationship. Others stress the four principles outlined below:

- *Appropriate attitude* — IK researchers need to be self-critical and must recognize their own bias toward formal scientific, urban, high-tech knowledge. It is the responsibility of the IK researcher to remember that IK systems may be just as valid or useful or that a low-tech solution can be highly appropriate.

- *Appropriate methods* — The researcher must ensure that the research methods are tailored to people's cultures, abilities, and requirements and effectively represent local people's points of view.

- *Multiple methods* — IK research requires a mixture of techniques that together facilitate the collection of different types of data and help confirm or reject research findings through a process of crosschecking or triangulation. A good combination of methods can access knowledge concealed in cultural norms or political factors.

- *Broad participation* — Participation means involving women, men, and children of all classes and requires from both the researcher and the informants more than mere attendance or answering questions. One way to elicit the IK of a community is by participating in its work and leisure activities (Wickham 1993).

IK limitations

All knowledge systems have their limitations and weaknesses, and IK is no exception. Neither IK nor international science will be appropriate and accurate in all circumstances. In the same way that it has proven unwise to uncritically accept international science (for example, green-revolution technology), it would be unwise to accept all traditional knowledge as good practice or as sustainable practice. Indigenous peoples have at times mismanaged resources. For example, according to Gadgil et al. (1993), nomadic hunters and gatherers who are not tied to any specific resource base may not have a conservation ethic. Some IK practices are less

> "Wise and unwise environmental practices and valid and invalid environmental beliefs coexist in many cultures. To assume differently is to assume that with respect to natural resource management indigenous peoples are either inherently superior or inherently inferior to the cultures of the developed world. Both of these extreme images — noble or ignoble savage — connote prejudice and do not serve the needs of development planners."
>
> *Source: Johannes (1993, p. 37)*

Table 3. A research-framework summary for IK research.

From the IPR debate	• The community and the participants are advised of the benefits and drawbacks of the research activity • Informed consent is obtained from the community and from each individual • The community controls when, how, and by whom the information is used
From IUCN	• People and the environment are recognized as a "whole" • The process begins by asking good questions • Each action leads to reflection and learning • The approach is people centred
From social science research	• Interviews are carefully designed to minimize errors • Great care is taken with the forward and back translation of terms and concepts
From gender research	• Women and men are trained as community researchers • Women are consulted on the design of the research process (the who, when, where, and how of conducting interviews) • The knowledge of women and men is collected • Data are disaggregated by gender and often by age • Women's confidential information is reported back to women, not men
From PRA	• Villagers (rich and poor, literate and nonliterate, young and old, women and men) participate in the research design, data analysis, and follow-up decisions • Researchers are facilitators and learners; they bring correct behaviour and attitude to the research process • The research is interactive and participatory, supporting the independence and the dignity of participants; it uses local languages, indigenous categories, and multiple, creative techniques (with a balance of group and individual techniques) • Data are visually shared; the information is created and owned by villagers; the knowledge stays in the village
From IK research	• Multiple, culturally appropriate methods that encourage broad participation (on the part of the participant and the researcher) are used • Researchers bring an appropriate attitude and an awareness of their own scientific bias • The 3 *R*s (respect, reciprocity, relationship) are maintained

Note: IUCN, International Union for the Conservation of Nature and Natural Resources; PRA, participatory rural appraisal.

efficient than modern technologies. IK can be less precise, as international science can measure or statistically verify phenomena to a high level of precision. Indigenous farmers' experiments can be poorly designed. Practices benign under conditions of low population may no longer be appropriate. IK can be incomplete or incorrect (McCorkle 1989, cited in Wickham 1993).

Johannes (1993) summarized the full gamut of things to expect by stating that some cultures clearly possess a traditional conservation ethic; other cultures apparently perceive little or no relationship between their activities and the state of their environment; and others had a traditional conservation ethic, but that has been compromised by external influences.

As stated at the beginning of this section, IK research methodology has borrowed and benefited from the input of a number of disciplines. Table 3 summarizes some of the key inputs relevant to establishing an ethical, reflective, participatory, and gender-sensitive IK research framework.

SECTION 4

Data Collection

Techniques for collecting IK should document what people do and why, within the larger framework of what they know and think (Brookfield 1996). PRA methods can reveal the hidden complexity of IK systems, but it is important to have a good sequencing of activities and an overall relaxed approach. Villagers may need time to assess the researcher as a person; the researcher may need time to change his or her attitudes and behaviour to match that of villagers (Emery 1997).

The techniques can yield an excessive amount of information, not all of it useful. Although the task of documentation is perceived as technically the easiest, it can be laborious, time-consuming, costly, and sometimes disappointing (Adugna 1996). It is important to have clear research objectives (that is, good questions) and some knowledge of the subject area. Johannes (1993) explained that the researcher should be able to determine whether the information is new, already well known, or implausible and, most importantly, be able to highlight the potentially significant points.

> "The successful collection of indigenous knowledge is dependent on the manner in which the information is collected, the relations established during the process, and the way the collection process is tailored to fit with the development priorities of the community in question."
>
> *Source: Maundu (1995)*

Thirty-one research techniques are described below (Mascarenhas et al. 1991, cited in Wickham 1993). (The techniques are not listed in any specific order.) Their application is illustrated in the case studies in Section 5. These techniques can be adapted to a particular research setting. The set of techniques one chooses for a research activity should answer IUCN's (1997) two core questions — How are the people? How is the ecosystem? — from a past, present, and future (current trends) perspective. A combination of group and individual techniques is suggested to overcome PRA's limitations.

The field situation will shape and test the methods and tools. This list of research techniques is not exhaustive, and as the discipline matures, field personnel will develop new and innovative research techniques. IIED (1994), IIRR (1996), and Narayan (1996) give more-in-depth descriptions of particular techniques.

Some PRA techniques

- *Review of secondary data* — Secondary data are analyzed to a large extent, but too much emphasis on previous analyses and opinions can mislead investigators.

> "Some research results and fragments of people's knowledge become current and are frequently quoted from one report to another. They become a common store of knowledge in international circles; but even then, the selection of approved knowledge goes through tight sieves which prejudice and reshape the local knowledge in a way which suits the economic and theoretical systems of outsiders."
>
> *Source: Kinyunyu and Swantz (1996, p. 62)*

- *Direct observation* — Observations are related to questions: What? When? Where? Who? Why? How?

- *Do it yourself* — Villagers are encouraged to teach the researcher how to do various activities. The researcher will learn how much skill and strength are required to do day-to-day rural activities, gaining an insider's perspective on a situation. Roles are reversed: villagers are the "experts" and attitudes are challenged.

- *Participatory mapping and modeling* — Using local materials, villagers draw or model current or historical conditions. The researcher then interviews the villager by "interviewing the map." This technique can be used to show watersheds, forests, farms, home gardens, residential areas, soils, water sources, wealth rankings, household assets, land-use patterns, changes in farming practices, constraints, trends, health and welfare conditions, and the distribution of various resources.

> According to Maundu (1995), the transect and guided field-walk method has several disadvantages. It is tiring, especially for older people, who tend to be most knowledgeable, time-consuming, and only effective in species-rich areas and heterogeneous habitats.

- *Transect walks and guided field walks* — The researcher and key informants conduct a walking tour through areas of interest to observe, to listen, to identify different zones or conditions, and to ask questions to identify problems and possible solutions. With this method, the outsider can quickly learn about topography, soils, land use, forests, watersheds, and community assets.

- *Seasonal calendars* — Variables such as rainfall, labour, income, expenditures, debt, animal fodder or pests, and harvesting periods can be drawn (or created with stones, seeds, and sticks) to show month-to-month variations and seasonal constraints and to highlight opportunities for action. An 18-month calendar can better illustrate variations than a 12-month calendar.

- *Daily-activity profiles* — Researchers can explore and compare the daily-activity patterns of men, women, youth, and elders by charting the amount of time taken to complete tasks.

- *Semistructured interviewing* — A semistructured interviewing and listening technique uses some predetermined questions and topics but allows new topics to be pursued as the interview develops. The interviews are informal and conversational but carefully controlled.

- *Types, sequencing, and chain interviews* — Individual, pair, and group interviews are combined in a sequence to take advantage of key informants and specialist groups.

- *Permanent-group interviews* — Established groups, farmers' groups, or people using the same water source can be interviewed together. This technique can help identify collective problems or solutions.

- *Time lines* — Major historical community events and changes are dated and listed. Understanding the cycles of change can help communities focus on future actions and information requirements.

- *Local histories* — Local histories are similar to time lines but give a more detailed account of how things have changed or are changing. For example, histories can be developed for crops, population changes, community health trends and epidemics, education changes, road developments, and trees and forests.

- *Local researchers and village analysts* — With some training, local people can conduct the research process (for example, collect, analyze, use, and present data; conduct transects; interview other villagers; draw maps; make observations).

- *Venn diagrams* — To show the relationship between things, overlapping circles are used to represent people, villages, or institutions; lines are added to reflect inputs and outputs.

- *Participatory diagraming* — People are encouraged to display their knowledge on pie and bar charts and flow diagrams.

- *Wealth and well-being rankings* — People are asked to sort cards (or slips of paper) representing individuals or households from rich to poor or from sick to healthy. This technique can be used for crosschecking information and for initiating discussions on a specific topic (for example, poverty). The technique can also be used to produce a benchmark against which future development interventions can be measured or evaluated.

- *Direct-matrix pair-wise ranking and scoring* — Direct-matrix pair-wise ranking and scoring is a tool used to discover local attitudes on various topics. People rank and compare individual items, using their own categories and criteria, by raising hands or placing representative objects on a board. For example, six different shrubs can be ranked from best to worst for their fuel, fodder, and erosion-control attributes. Other resources can be ranked in terms of taste or marketability. Wealth ranking can be used to identify wealth criteria and establish the relative position of households.

- *Matrices* — Matrices can be used to gather information and to facilitate or focus analyses and discussions. For example, a problem–opportunity matrix could have columns with the following labels: soil type, land use, cropping patterns, and available resources; and rows with the following labels: problems, constraints, local solutions, and initiatives already tried.

- *Traditional management systems and local-resource collections* — Local people collect samples (for example, of soils, plants). This can be an efficient way to learn about the local biodiversity, management systems, and taxonomies.

- *Portraits, profiles, case studies, and stories* — Household histories or stories of how a certain conflict was resolved are recorded. This can provide short but insightful descriptions of characteristic problems and how they are dealt with.

- *Key probes* — A question addressing a key issue is asked of different informants, and the answers are compared. The question might be something like "If my goat enters your field and eats your crops, what do you and I do?"

- *Folklore, songs, poetry, and dance* — Local folklore, songs, dance, and poetry are analyzed to provide insight into values, history, practices, and beliefs.

- *Futures possible* — People are asked how they would like things to be in 1 year and to predict what will happen if nothing is done or if something is done. People's desires, wishes, and expectations are revealed.

- *Diagrams exhibition* — Diagrams, maps, charts, and photos of the research activity are displayed in a public place to share information, facilitate discussions, and provide an additional crosschecking device. The exhibition can inspire other villagers to take part in research activities.

- *Shared presentations and analysis* — Participants are encouraged to present their findings to other villagers and to outsiders, providing another opportunity for crosschecking, feedback, comment, and criticism.

- *Night halts* — The researchers live in the village during the research process. This facilitates all interactions between the outsiders and the villagers, invites change in the outsiders' attitudes, and allows for early-morning and evening discussions, when villagers tend to have more leisure time.

- *Short questionnaires* — Short and issue-specific questionnaires can be useful if conducted late in the research process.

- *Field report writing* — Key findings are recorded before "leaving" the village. (This assumes that the community has consented to having the research data leave the village.) Brief summaries are made of each diagram, model, and map, as well as of the process involved in creating them.

- *Self-correcting field notes* — Field notes help the researcher remain focused on what has been done, what was learned through the exercise, and what needs to be done. Rereading the field notes on a regular basis helps the researcher correct errors and identify problems and solutions.

- *Survey of villagers' attitudes toward PRA* — To improve the PRA process and techniques and maintain realistic expectations, the researcher asks the villagers what they expected and what they learned from the PRA research process.

- *Intriguing practices and beliefs* — Indigenous practices and beliefs are noted, even if they are based on myth or superstition. Even practices that are unusual or don't fit in with conventional scientific think-ing are worth exploring because they are meaningful to local people.

> In some places in Africa, seeds dipped in blood are used as an offering to spirits.
>
> *Source: Unknown*

Case Studies

Four cases studies are summarized below. Together, they demonstrate a range of research frameworks, objectives, and techniques.

A case study from Indonesia

To avoid a requirement for foreign or new approaches to sustainable development, an IK research project in Indonesia (Wickham 1993) used PRA techniques to highlight the contribution that could be made by using local approaches that already support sustainable development.

The setting was a small, isolated Hindu village of 90 households in an upland agricultural area with steep ridges and sloping terraces, in Bali. The residents had little access to formal education and agricultural extension services and very limited exposure to modern technologies. The area received 2 680 mm of rain per year; 97% of the land was devoted to dryland farming and agroforestry. Subsistence crops included corn, peanuts, cassava, dry rice, sweet potato, and bananas; cash crops included cloves, vanilla, coffee, salak, durian, oranges, and jackfruit. Most households had two or three cows and some chickens and pigs; a few households also raised ducks and geese. There was a (small) trend away from labour-intensive, subsistence crops to cash crops. Land tenure was a mixture of state lands, lands controlled and cultivated by residents without title, and private lands.

The field research was conducted over a 4-month period, in 1991 and 1992. The Canadian researcher and his Balinese assistant lived with the village leader and his wife. Thirty villagers — nine men, nine women, six boys, and six girls — participated in the research. The participants were 10–70 years old; some were illiterate, and others were high-school graduates. A number of other individuals contributed their knowledge through casual discussions.

The researchers used two main PRA techniques, mapping and resource collections, with several other techniques (see Table 4). The PRA techniques produced a large quantity of information. However, much IK remained undiscovered and unobserved. The study collected information from 30 participants, so the results cannot be said to reflect the knowledge of other individuals. Also, some of the information was unverified. The researchers worked with individuals rather than groups to avoid raising local expectations about what the research might yield for the commu-nity. This limited the amount of group brainstorming and triangulation.

> Researchers should self-test and pretest any techniques that are new to them.
>
> *Source: Wickham (1993)*

PRA research strategy

To become familiar with the setting, the researchers constructed six maps and one transect before beginning any other investigation. They learned more about the mapped areas by using other PRA techniques (see Table 4, column 2).

Fifteen villagers completed 10 village maps: 5 village area maps and 5 farm sketches. On 1 m × 0.5 m paper, these mapmakers used felt markers to sketch topography, slope, hydrology, crops, trees, soil types, eroded sites, soil- and water-conservation practices, land tenure, social enterprises, roads, houses, and buildings. A map legend, using simple symbols and local terminologies, had been prepared to assist the mapmakers. Mapping sessions took place in the field and lasted 1–2 hours. This included time for the researchers to take a pre-mapping walk with the participant, time for the mapmakers to sketch, and time for the researchers to interview the mapmakers about the contents of the map. The researchers learned more about the mapped areas by using the PRA tech-niques listed in column 1 of Table 4. During the drawing process, partici-

> In Wickham's (1993) experience, PRA methodology accessed people's beliefs and knowledge about their local environment and how they use this knowledge to live. PRA techniques facilitated and enabled the participation of men, women, girls, and boys; the meth-ods enabled the participants to explain practices, beliefs, concepts, and ideas using their own terminol-ogy and examples.

pants had to be reassured that absolute precision was not expected. The reli-ability and quality of the villagers' maps were a function of how comfortable the mapmakers were with drawing with felt markers.

In addition, the researchers hired eight community researchers — two men, two woman, two girls, and two boys — to collect three major village resources: samples of the tree species, bamboo varieties, and soil types. The eight participants collected as many of these resources as possible.

Direct-matrix ranking and intriguing practices and beliefs were the techniques used during the postcollection sessions to learn more from the villagers about the use, availability, and characteristics of the collected samples. The resource inventories were time-efficient and cost-effective. Each village researcher took 1–3 hours to collect the samples. Children proved to have considerable knowledge of local resource practices and were not as wary of the research process. After collection, the researchers spent an additional 2–3 hours to interview each participant and record the information. In all, 70 hours was spent on collecting, identifying, and recording information on 298 samples. The village leader had suggested that a fee per sample be given to the participants (total cost 10 CAD); and this proved sufficient to attract participants.

Wickham (1993) commented that it had been a challenge to sustain a participatory approach. Occasionally, it had been difficult to "let-go" and not direct the process. It had also been a challenge to focus on "process" rather than "product." For instance, getting the map drawn or the resource collection completed was not the objective. Rather, the objective was to use the map and collections as a catalyst or interviewing tool to learn more about specific practices and beliefs.

Table 4. PRA techniques used in the Indonesian case study.

Participatory mapping	Researchers' transect and mapping exercise	Resource collections	Supplementary research techniques
Direct observation	Direct observation	Direct-matrix ranking	Review of secondary data
Semistructured interviewing	Semistructured interviewing	Intriguing practices and beliefs	Do it yourself
Portraits, profiles case studies, and stories	Portraits, profiles case studies, and stories		Time lines
Key probes	Key probes		Night halts
Folklore			Self-correcting field notes
Futures possible			
Intriguing practices and beliefs			

Note: PRA, participatory rural appraisal. These techniques are described in Section 4.

Research results

The researchers summarized the emic findings — villagers' knowledge, techniques, beliefs, and practices. Villagers identified 146 tree types and their various uses for firewood, construction, ceremonies, crafts, tools, and medicines. Villagers also identified 10 species of bamboo and 8 soil types, using local taxonomies.

To limit soil erosion, farmers used a combination of techniques — they maintained vegetation cover, cut terraces, practiced strip cultivation, and planted perennials and annuals together. They used green manures and mulching for soil-fertility management. The farmers' techniques for managing weeds included multiple cropping with fallow, mulching, and selective weeding. They used air guns for animal pests, such as squirrels.

The use of tree resources was controlled by a community belief system. Several of the supernatural beliefs were associated with sacred areas, cemeteries, and areas near temples. The fear of spiritual or financial penalties or community sanctions prevented those trees from being cut. Other practices followed a calendar. For instance, according to local convention, wood and bamboo could only be harvested every sixth day. When a tree was harvested, people complied with the customary practice of planting one tree for each tree cut. Villagers were sometimes unable to provide an explanation for their following a practice.

Discussion

The researchers compared villager resource knowledge with available (etic) scientific data. Villagers identified 146 tree types; biologists from a nearby university had identified 16. Although the village tree inventory was probably inflated — different spellings and different uses resulted in different names — by any criteria, villager knowledge of tree types was considerable. Villagers identified and classified eight soil types; Western science identified only one soil group. Local farmers distinguished their soils by colour, texture, and seasonal characteristics (for example, wet, dry). Wickham (1993) concluded that villager descriptive knowledge for trees, bamboo, and soil resources was, at the very least, equivalent to, and likely more detailed than, corresponding data from trained scientific researchers.

The researchers compared the village farm-management techniques with the principles of sustainable agriculture and found the village techniques to be characteristic of low-external-input and sustainable agriculture. Villagers managed the soil and maintained crop health by imitating local ecological processes. The indigenous beliefs and practices were examined in relation to people's resource use and conservation. The beliefs associated with the use of trees and animals placed temporary or permanent restrictions on their use. An informal system of religious and spiritual taboos, the local customs, and the fear of community sanctions supported a conservation ethic and were sufficient to regulate people's resource use. The villagers needed no formal policing or enforcement mechanism.

Wickham (1993) concluded that

- The farmers maintained a sustainable agricultural production level, sufficient to meet local needs;

- People used their own local capacities (that is, knowledge of resources and ecological processes) to make rational socioeconomic decisions; and

- The community used culturally relevant mechanisms to prevent excessive resource use.

A case study from Ecuador

IK research has often been carried out by outsiders for other outsiders, with the result that the content, language, and storage location of the data made the research findings inaccessible to the local communities. By way of contrast, this Ecuadorian case study (Kothari 1995) is an account of how local people compiled a book of their oral knowledge of medicinal plants.

It took 10 months to complete the book (3 months to do the research; 7 months to prepare the book). An NGO representing 18 communities from the region provided administrative support. Following the presentation of the project objectives, the 18 communities were formally invited to participate in the project. Each community was asked to select two literate participants, one female and one male. The project coordinators (three NGO members, a locally respected healer, and the author) offered 10 USD per month, to attract participants; the total budget was 2 000 USD. Six of the 18 communities expressed an interest, but initially the majority were unable to find a female participant. In some cases, the younger women's parents or husbands worried about mixed- gender issues. Older women did not meet the literacy requirement, but they willingly participated once the literacy requirement was relaxed. Ultimately, the project team included the project coordinators and six men and six women from various villages.

The coordinators developed a short, bilingual questionnaire to obtain the following information about the medicinal plants and their uses: symptoms and causes of illness, the corresponding plant remedy, a description of the plant and its habitat, its local name(s), the method for preparing and administrating the remedy, and the plant's nonmedical uses. Other questions helped to identify the traditional healers. The coordinators trained the 12 participants to administer the questionnaire by pairing them up and asking them to interview and document one another's knowledge of medicinal plants. This pretested and improved the wording of the questionnaire. Most important, it provided the participants with an opportunity to gain hands-on experience with an unfamiliar exercise, both as interviewers and interviewees. Following the training session, the participants selected the interviewees, usually from their own community, and completed the questionnaires in their preferred language.

All the participants met once a week to discuss their experiences and to review the completed questionnaires. Important project decisions, such as addressing individual concerns, planning the direction of the project, dealing with financial matters, and setting a target number of questionnaires to be completed per week, were made collectively. At the end of the interviewing phase, the budget was exhausted. Seven of the initial participants (five of them women) continued with the project. In the postinterview phase, the collected information was sorted by plant species. If there was consensus on a particular plant remedy, the participants summarized the data. Remedies for which there was no consensus were laid aside for further investigation.

Kothari designed the book for the villagers. The information is presented in a structured but simple format, in both Spanish and the local language. The book presents the preparation and administration of each remedy in written and pictorial form. A drawing of the plant and its local name are also given. Four hundred copies of the book were presented to the participating communities. The intent is to have all proceeds from the sale of the book support related activities.

A case study from Ethiopia

The research objectives of this Ethiopian case study (Abbink 1995) were to inventory the most important medicinal plants used by three different groups and to establish whether the groups use the same plants or influence each other in the adoption and use of certain plants. Observation was the key approach because many people refused at first to reveal which plants were used for healing rites and other ritual purposes. Initially, information was gathered as part of a larger, 14-month project. The second phase involved identifying and interviewing specialists on plants and plant use and organizing small gathering expeditions to certain areas. This was done with two local assistants. The third phase, during which local people collect plants, give details on their use, and answer a questionnaire, is still in progress. Four local, experienced field assistants were hired for this phase. Because the assistants were previously trained and were living among their own people, the author expects to obtain reliable and detailed information. The author supervises the work during brief visits every 6 months. Trials to compare the effects of traditional and modern medicines are being considered.

A case study from Venezuela

The objectives of this Venezuelan research project (Melnyk 1995) were to gain an understanding of and quantify the value of gathered forest foods and to document the extent to which wild plant and animal foods contribute to household nutrition. The researcher compared a small village (17 inhabitants) with a larger village (350 inhabitants), which had less access to forest resources, to analyze the effects that permanent settlement, population growth, and deforestation have on the availability, use, and management of forest foods. Data were collected through direct observation, interviews, time-allocation studies, and measurements of the amounts of wild forest products collected and eaten. In 1992/93, the researcher spent alternate months in each village for a period of 13 consecutive months (so that seasonal variations could be observed).

The local people recognized as edible 131 forest plant species, 21 mammals, 25 birds, 57 fish, 15 reptiles, 2 amphibians, 13 anthropods, and 2 annelids. Despite the scarcity of forest resources and the permanence of the settlement, the larger village maintained the collection of forest plants in a manner similar to that of the smaller village. In the larger village, the sampled households collected 968 kilograms of forest plant products over 71 days of direct observation, whereas in the smaller village, the households collected 405 kilograms over 87 days. The inhabitants of the larger village spent more time on average (181 person–minutes) harvesting forest products than the people from the smaller village did (86 person–minutes). The marketable portion of the village harvest had a local value of 2 557 USD. Extrapolated to a full year, the annual average value of the forest food was about 3 300 USD per household. People from the larger village often sold forest fruits in the local market, with a day's collection of palm fruits averaging 9.88 USD. A day labourer working the same number of hours earned 7.62 USD.

Melnyk (1995) concluded that forest foods provided both villages with dietary nutrients, particularly protein and fats. Seasonal changes allowed one product to be replaced by another, ensuring that there was something to eat throughout the year.

Assessing, Validating, and Experimenting with IK

An "egg of sustainability" metaphor developed by IUCN (1997) — with the yolk representing people and the white representing the ecosystem — captures the essence of sustainable development. The image succinctly expresses the human–ecosystem interrelationships and the need to assess human and ecosystem well-being together — the whole system as well as the parts. A society is thought to be sustainable when both the human condition and the condition of the ecosystem are satisfactory or improving. The system improves only when both the condition of the ecosystem and the human condition improve. One objective of IK research is to improve the well-being of people and their ecosystems and to move toward more sustainable human–ecosystem combinations.

Depending on the scope and the breadth of the research project, multiple PRA tools (see Section 4) will have generated data to answer two fundamental questions — How are the people? How is their ecosystem? — or people–environment data to answer a more specific IK question. The researcher and the community will have an outsider's and an insider's picture of the ecosystem components (for example, the land, water, soil, air, biodiversity, and resources) and the human-system components (for example, wealth, livelihood, health, population, and knowledge). The state of each component, how and why it has changed over time, who caused the change, and who benefited or suffered from the change should have been identified. During the data-collection phase, interesting IK systems and technologies will have been identified and observed. Users will have been interviewed. The community, with the assistance of the IK researchers, will have identified its own questions or problems in relation to some aspect of the IK data, as well as, perhaps, some options for solving some specific problems.

> "Western science has been slow to develop methods to assess complex systems. ... analyses have focussed on outputs — milk production, meat production — and neglected the benefits of local breeds, which thrive on minimal inputs."
>
> Source: IIRR (1996, pp. 122–123)

Despite the recent focus on IK, development projects still appear to make little use of it. In part, this is due to the fact that less attention has been placed on methods for assessing, evaluating, and using IK information.

Sustainable-development assessment criteria

The key to assessment is asking the right questions. Assessment is a process that requires assessment criteria and data interpretation — selecting criteria and relevant indicators, collecting relevant indicator data, and analyzing the data — a process dependant on asking the right questions from the onset. It seems reasonable to assess IK

> "A sentimental belief in 'traditional values' and a gut feeling that the 'people know best' without knowing why and under what circumstances, will be equally unhelpful and damaging to the prospects of rural development in the long run."
>
> *Source: Richards (1980), cited in Wickham (1993, p. 29)*

systems and technologies against sustainable development and productivity criteria. But whose criteria and whose interpretation should be used in this assessment?

Productivity criteria can serve to illustrate this point. Productivity is defined as the capacity to produce, and yield is the amount produced. The spread of monocultures of high-yielding varieties and fast-growing species in forestry and agriculture has been justified on grounds of increased productivity. However, the corporate sector uses very narrow indicators to define yield and productivity. Productivity and total yield of monocultures are high in terms of one product. High-yield plantations, for instance, pick one tree species for yields of one part of the tree (for example, pulpwood). Productivity may mean one thing for a paper corporation and a different thing for a farmer who needs fodder and green manure. Similarly, plant improvement in agriculture has been based on improving the yield of a desired product. But what is unwanted by agribusinesses may be wanted by the poor.

The productivity and total yield of monocultures are low in the context of diverse outputs and needs. Overall, productivity, total yield, and sustainability are much higher in mixed systems of farming and forestry. A poor farmer may define a productive farm as one that produces crops, fish, chickens, livestock, clothing, shelter, and medicine. According to Shiva (1995a), productivity based on uniformity (monocultures) threatens biodiversity conservation and sustainability and eventually threatens a collapse in yields, because monocultures are ecologically unstable and invite diseases and pests.

Ultimately, the farmer decides what is productive for his or her farm, adopting and rejecting options on the basis of his or her own questions ("How can I survive?"), criteria, and indicators. Unlike the person in the corporate sector, who stresses the question "How can I make more money?," a farmer may also emphasize production stability. In drought-prone areas, for instance, low-yield varieties that are guaranteed to produce every year reduce risk and may be selected over (or along with) improved varieties that may be more vulnerable to drought.

The productivity example highlights the fact that assessment criteria and the indicators used in evaluation can be international, national, or local; quantitative or qualitative; economic (market or indigenous economy), social, or ecological; and combinations thereof. Mazzucato (1997) argued that if we are to understand the forms of economic organization in other societies, it's time to look at indigenous economies in terms of indigenous criteria. To date, economic studies have based their analyses on Western economic concepts. Inputs and outputs are largely defined and assessed in terms of material goods and money. Land valuation is still dominated by the Western concept of private property. In general, *the more the better* concept dominates economic definitions of rational objectives. Mazzucato asserted that it is time to examine whether economic terms, such as benefits, costs, insurance, interest, security, and risk, have the same meaning at a local level. By doing so, researchers would gain a better understanding of why farmers do what they do.

At the international level, there is no consensus on the criteria and indicators for sustainable development. There is agreement on the need to develop country-, region-, and sector-specific indicators and criteria. At the local level, numerous case studies (some presented later in this section) illustrate that the relative importance of criteria and the actual criteria and indicators used vary with each site and each specific technology. This suggests that to understand human behaviour and action, one needs to identify the questions a given action relates to. It also suggests a need to keep criteria and indicators under review and to examine, test, and begin to experiment with different indicators. Furthermore, it is important to ensure that criteria and indicators developed at the national and local levels are not contradictory and that any necessary trade-offs, such as between social and ecological goals, are transparent and clearly stated.

Benfer and Furbee (1996) stated that it is not essential that IK be validated by scientific criteria. They argued that anthropologists validate models of IK through intensive interviews and through observation of those who hold those beliefs. Without denying this, the discussion that follows assumes that good IK assessment and experimentation will tap both the insider's and the outsider's questions and assessments. As Van Crowder (1996) remarked, innovations for sustainable development will reflect the interactions among different actors with complementary contributions to offer.

One way to look at integrating insider and outsider perspectives on assessment is to analyze failures encountered in technology-transfer projects. Four case studies are pre-

Research in the Canadian North has shown that hunters and scientists may apply the same ecological indicators in their evaluation of the local environment (for example, age, sex, health of animal populations). Western science and traditional environmental knowledge diverge mostly in their explanations or interpretations of ecological processes and in their concepts of environmental management.

Source: DCI (1991)

sented here. The project focus in the first three cases was on ecological factors, reflecting a narrowly defined concept of sustainable development that ignored social considerations. The fourth case, also a failure, highlights some institutional factors of relevance to sustainable development.

A case study from Thailand

The rate at which farmers adopt soil-conservation practices remains low in Thailand. In this study (Pahlman 1995), most farmers thought that soil erosion was not serious enough to require action. The farmers' primary concerns were weeds, insect pests, and water shortages. When asked, farmers stated that the decline in soil quality was due to a land shortage, making fallowing and soil regeneration impossible. Farmers' views were sought on soil-conservation measures. Most farmers regarded the integration of trees, particularly "economic" fruit trees, to be the most effective and suitable measure. Although the majority of farmers were aware that tree crops have beneficial effects on soil quality, soil conservation did not seem to be a major incentive to plant trees. Farmers wanted to grow trees for economic reasons, to suppress weed growth, and to offset the effects of deforestation (for example, dwindling timber and forest food supplies). The study confirmed that if sustainable land use is to be achieved in the upland areas, emphasis must be placed on practices that also meet other needs — notably, food and income. Pahlman concluded that there is no point trying to promote sustainable farming practices on the grounds of conservation alone, when farmers themselves see their problems differently.

A case study from Peru

A case study from Peru (MacMillan 1995) showed that farmers were reluctant to invest in farming alternatives because of the high start-up costs. The author concluded that farmers will invest in alternatives only if economic returns are likely to materialize within 1 year.

A case study from the Philippines

In this case study from the Philippines (Fujisaka et al. 1993), technology transfer failed because a single part of the farmers' circumstances — heavier soil texture — made the plowing technology too labour intensive and too difficult to operate. The lesson from this study is that efforts should be taken to verify that any technology to be transferred will indeed be compatible with the new environment, even if the receiving farmers are operating under what appears to be the same conditions as those where the technology was successful.

A case study from India

Before government intervention, villagers in this case study from India (Agrawal 1993) drew their water from the local feudal lord's deep well. Two or three people were employed to draw water and distribute it among the families, and these employees maintained the necessary equipment (rope, barrels, buckets, pulley) and draught animals. Each household paid the employees a fixed amount, based on household water use. All the villagers depended on this well for their drinking water. The government then provided the village with a storage tank to hold piped water from a tube well 6 kilometres away. Now, more than enough free water is available (that is, the storage tank overflows) for 8–10 days of the month; water supply is adequate for 5–6 days; and for about 15 days each month, water supply is insufficient. Why? The government employee in charge of operating the tube well is negligent: he forgets to turn the valve on or off, does not do repair and maintenance work in a timely way, and occasionally sells the diesel fuel that is supposed to be used to run the motor. To remedy this, it was suggested that each house pay a small fee (but far less than what was paid in the old barrels-and-buckets system) to hire someone to watch over the government employee. However, the more affluent villagers are unwilling to pay for this service because they have cisterns — they can store water whenever the supply is abundant and would gain nothing from a regular water supply. The poor, on the other hand, have come to depend on the government employee.

Under the old system, all the villagers depended on the feudal lord's well and found it to their advantage to ensure that water from the well was distributed equitably. People not paying their share could be prevented from using the water. Although the new system is technically more efficient — providing more water and at a lower per-unit cost — the government implemented it without considering issues of people's participation and institutional design. In fact, the new arrangements encouraged the breakdown of indigenous participatory institutions; some villagers were worse off under the new system. Depending on their assets and incomes, some groups of people may receive more benefits from a seemingly equitable intervention than other groups of people: though water was available to all the villagers for free, those with their own personal cisterns gained greater benefits.

One of the most notable lessons from this case is a strong reminder to assess the impact of interventions on local institutions and equity and to adopt the point of view of different groups of people in the village — rather than treating the village as a homogeneous unit.

Summarizing case-study findings

Each case study documenting a failure helps to highlight how insiders assess their well-being. Many case studies similar to those presented above have contributed to our understanding of sustainable-development and technology-transfer issues. Fujisaka et al. (1993), Pahlam (1995), Puffer (1995), Titilola (1995), Wilk (1995), IIRR (1996), and others have showed that innovations that become permanent local knowledge and "working solutions" often have several features in common. An ecologically sound option is more likely to be adopted or, to put it another way, be assessed positively and be sustainable at the local level if it

- Is suitable for the local physical environment;

- Addresses farmer-identified problems and constraints;

- Reduces risk;

- Meets multiple needs;

- Generates income;

- Provides acceptable economic returns;

- Is affordable;

- Uses locally available skills, tools, and materials (spare parts, fuels, or ingredients);

- Saves labour;

To reintroduce animals to some farms in the Philippines, IIRR adapted a traditional livestock-distribution scheme. In the traditional practice, an animal's off- spring are shared between the animal's owner and the animal's caretaker. If a cow produces 10 calves, the owner gets 5 and the caretaker gets 5. The cow is returned to the owner at the end of the production period. Under the IIRR scheme, IIRR grants livestock to a local farmer's cooperative, which turns them over to cooperative members for caretaking. The caretakers get the second, fourth, and subsequent offspring; the first and third offspring go to the cooperative, which assigns them to other members on the waiting list. Caretakers become owners of the assigned animal after 3–5 years. The modified traditional scheme has worked very well.

Source: IIRR (1996)

- Is efficient (for example, increases yields);

- Is easy to understand;

- Produces visible results within a reasonable amount of time;

- Can be maintained by existing organizations;

- Fits into, minimizes disruption of, or modifies (rather than replacing) existing practices;

- Fits existing systems of ownership, obligation, and authority;

- Affects different groups equitably;

- Is supported by trusted sources (for example, relatives);

- Is culturally appropriate and does not challenge or contradict fundamental cultural beliefs; and

- Takes into consideration local preferences, such as taste and beliefs about nutrition.

Practices that fetch low economic returns may perform social functions or conserve the environment. In other words, assessment of IK must recognize the context in which the technology was developed and is applied and the criteria by which local people assess their own IK. IIRR (1996) suggests that from local people we can find out the following: what they value most in a specific IK; why they chose it; what they see as its strengths and weaknesses; what would happen and who would be most affected if the IK were not available; and what features they look for when they test a technology. "Only if we combine both insider's and outsider's assessment, will we be able to identify and better understand the value and usefulness of IK."

Source: IIRR (1996, p. 123)

Indicators

A significant aspect of the assessment process will be identifying appropriate, pertinent, verifiable, somewhat quantifiable indicators that can be effectively measured against the relevant criteria. In commenting on desertification indicators, Krugmann (1996) noted that indicators tend to occur in a hierarchy, from microindicators to macroindicators, reflecting perspectives, experiences, processes, and actions (questions) at different levels. Indicators can be quantitative or qualitative: quantitative indicators are easier to measure and to aggregate, whereas qualitative indicators are better at capturing the complexity of changing situations. Indicators can be direct or indirect (erosion gullies versus charcoal price), descriptive (status of the environment), or performance oriented (measured against some benchmark). Indicators also have a time horizon, with some more relevant to the short, medium, or long term. Depending on the type of project, monitoring of some indicators may be needed from the start of the project until long after the project's completion to allow the full impact of the project to be observed. Indicators can also reflect change or signal change in variables.

Grassroots indicators

Rural communities have local sets of indicators that they use to monitor and evaluate their environmental quality and to predict environmental change. Often, communities attach different values to different indicators; they use the ones they consider more reliable to plan and schedule their production activities and to help them make decisions for their survival strategies. Mwadime (1996) noted that in a Kenyan community, it took a combination of indicators to influence farmers' planning and decision-making.

Some examples of grassroots indicators are the appearance and behaviour of flora and fauna (in particular, the flowering or sprouting schedule of key plants and the arrival and activity of birds, insects, frogs, and toads), wind patterns or changes in the direction of wind flow, and the position of star groups. Such indicators help the people detect changes in seasonal patterns, predict the rains or the ending of seasons, identify soil fertility, and monitor the state of the environment (Oduol 1996). The behaviour of livestock and wildlife can indicate the nutritional value of the forage plants and the range; milk yields can indicate forage availability and quality. The mating frequency of animals, the texture and colour of dung, or the condition of an animal's fur can reflect environmental quality (Kipuri 1996).

Grassroots indicators are specific to a given ecological, cultural, social, and economic setting and to gender or age class (Krugmann 1996). The identification of grassroots indicators may entail a lengthy participatory process. The choice of insider and outsider indicators will depend on how clearly the indicators reveal the criteria in question and on whether the data can be obtained. The overall assessment may involve the weighing of hybrid indicators: combined outsider and insider indicators.

A screening form for sustainability

IUCN's two components — ecosystem and people — can be used to organize a screening form for assessing the sustainability of a system or given technology (Figure 2). This scheme can blend scientific criteria with those identified as important at the local level. It assumes that sustainable IK systems are not only ecologically sound but also attractive enough to be transferable and adoptable at the local level. The form should be completed by both insiders and outsiders, to obtain an overall assessment. IIRR (1996) sug-

> Scientific and indigenous criteria often have the same name (for example, cost-effectiveness) but differ in how they are measured (they have different indicators). More often, indigenous indicators are qualitative, reflecting a more holistic evaluation and a larger number of considerations. The researcher will have to cope with the different types of indicators.

gests that some of the techniques used for data collection, for instance, matrix ranking (see Section 4), can also be used by insiders for their assessment.

This screening form should be considered a work in progress. It will need to be adapted and improved for a specific application. Insiders and outsiders will need to select the criteria relevant to their specific evaluation and then select appropriate indicators for each criterion.

This screening-form approach can be used to identify an option's strengths and weaknesses. Once identified, these strengths and weaknesses can become the specific evaluation criteria for further experimentation and quantification. The approach assumes that a full description of the system or technology is available. One should note that a system or technology with only a few low-impact adverse effects is probably more sustainable and transferable than a system or technology with many adverse affects. However, if a system or technology has one significant adverse effect, this can indicate that it is unsustainable.

> This screening form is based on the Nunavut Environmental Impact Assessment procedures and the Canadian Environmental Impact Assessment procedures. While I was under contract with the Nunavut Board, one of my major tasks was integrating traditional knowledge into the Nunavut procedures. The screening form, as presented here, was revised for this purpose.

IUCN's Barometer of Sustainability

The screening form will highlight important issues, and this qualitative assessment may be sufficient to allow insiders and outsiders to make an informed decision about the next action. However, an overall understanding of how all

Indicate whether the system or technology has a negative (-), positive (+), or neutral (n) impact on the listed criteria.

Ecosystem

Biodiversity

- Wildlife diversity
- Rare or endangered species
- Species abundance
- Wild plant diversity
- Crop diversity
- Introduces exotic species? If yes, this could be a negative (-) impact.

Land

- Wildlife habitat
- Vegetation cover
- Soil texture
- Nutrient recycling
- Soil fertility
- Soil structure
- Soil or slope stability (e.g., erosion)

Water

- Water access
- Water supply
- Water quantity
- Water quality
- Drainage pattern

Air

- Air quality

Resource use

- Land use
- Conservation of natural resources
- Resource use

People

Human needs

- Diverse outputs (productivity)
- Food security
- Yield (efficiency)
- Risk
- Income or income distribution
- Capital requirements
- Economic return, profit margin
- Labour requirements
- Maintenance / learning requirements
- Self-reliance (uses local materials?)
- Control over output and process
- Living conditions (e.g., shelter)
- Human health (e.g., sanitation, toxicity)
- Energy supply (e.g., wood, fuel)

Social self-determination

- Family structure
- Gender roles
- Population growth
- Education
- Local institutions
- Local culture
- The rights of local communities
- Community health
- Local economy / capital flow
- Local (re)investment
- Community infrastructure (e.g., roads)
- Community harvesting
- Access to community resources (e.g., water, grazing lands)

- Community cultural landmarks
- Community recreational activities
- Land tenure

Equity Who benefits?

- Women
- Girls
- Old
- Poor
- Illiterate
- Men
- Boys
- Young
- Rich
- Literate

Questions (Yes = positive impact)

- Does the system or technology respond to problems and constraints identifed by villagers?
- Were local people involved in all stages of the project planning / development?
- Is the system or technology supported by the local power structure?
- Is the system or technology compatible with current local practices, preferences, and wisdom?
- Does the system or technology build on local practices and on existing capacity?
- Is the system or technology supported by other factors (e.g., land tenure, macro policy)?

Figure 2. A screening form for sustainability.

of these criteria and indicators are interacting is important. Each indicator represents a specific issue or criterion, but when many criteria are presented together, they may offer a conflicting and perhaps confusing picture of the sustainability of the IK system or technology being assessed. For instance, the technology may improve the water supply, but the water quality will deteriorate and many of the other criteria may be affected in a positive, neutral, or negative way.

To obtain a clearer understanding of the overall situation when dealing with multiple criteria and indicators, one might use the Barometer of Sustainability that Robert Prescott-Allen developed for IUCN to measure a society's well-being and progress toward sustainability. The barometer organizes and combines indicators from a wide range of issues or criteria into a two-dimensional index. The y-axis represents a combined index score for human well-being; the x-axis, a combined index score for ecosystem well-being. This two-dimensional index treats people and the environment as equally important. The lower score is read as the overall well-being or sustainability of the system. So, for example, an improvement in the ecosystem well-being at the expense of human well-being is made apparent, and the lower score for human well-being would be the overall index score.

With the barometer, each indicator is associated with its own performance scale using values appropriate to the issue or criterion. Only those indicators with values that can be interpreted as bad or good with respect to well-being can be used. A simple calculation is used to convert each indicator measurement into one of the five sectors of the 100-point scale: good, OK, medium, poor, or bad. All calculations are relatively easy, but the interested reader is advised to contact IUCN for a full documentation of the method.[3] The barometer can accommodate any hierarchical arrangement of criteria. (Figure 3 uses the "screening form for sustainability" criteria.)

It does not matter how many levels make up the hierarchy, as long as the subsystems are ecosystem and people. Individual scores for the indicators are combined up the hierarchy, from indicator, to criteria, to category, to subsystem, resulting in an index for people and an index for the ecosystem. The indicators on a particular level are combined — they are averaged when they are equally important, and they are weighted if they vary in importance. A critical indicator can be given a veto function.

The barometer results, along with an analysis of the key issues, will enable participants to draw conclusions about the conditions of people and

---

[3] "An Approach to Assessing Progress toward Sustainability — Tools and Training Series." IUCN Publication Services Unit, 219C Huntington Road, Cambridge CB 3 ODL, UK. Telephone: +44 1223 277894; fax: +44 1223 277175.

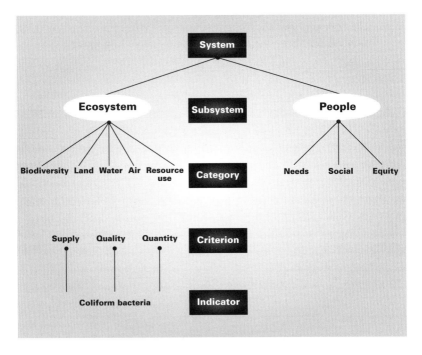

Figure 3. Summing indicators up on the IUCN Barometer of Sustainability hierarchy.

Note: This example shows a few criteria (water supply, quality, and quantity)
from the screening form for sustainability (see Figure 2), along with
a possible indicator (coliform bacteria).

their ecosystem in relation to the system under study. The barometer can also be used as a communication tool, allowing villagers to discuss where they are on each axis.

Comparative approaches to validation

The assessment of IK systems and technologies for sustainable development can be a very involved exercise, as outlined by the screening-form and barometer processes. Other research projects may have much narrower goals, for instance, a need to validate or experiment with a specific IK technology. The research, for instance, may have one or more of the following objectives:

- To validate the effectiveness of the technology or system (for example, increases in yield);

- To find out whether the technology or system can be adapted for other circumstances (for example, more intensive agriculture); or

- To determine if the efficiency of the technology or system can be improved for local use or transfer.

The simplest form of validation compares the results (yield or other desirable characteristics) of using the technology with the results of not using the technology. On-station and on-farm comparative testing can be used to determine whether it would be more practical and economic to use an indigenous innovation on its own or to combine it with a modern technology (Kakonge 1995). Comparative testing is also frequently used to differentiate between similar indigenous technologies.

When evaluating and comparing the effectiveness of IK systems, one also needs to identify the reasons for a particular practice or belief. For instance, if a farmer builds a stone wall in a particular location, rather than in the location that a scientific observer might predict, it may be that the stone wall would be washed away by heavy rains if placed in the predicted location (IIRR 1996).

An example from India illustrates the comparative procedure. Most Indian farmers put neem leaves in their grain-storage containers so that pests won't damage the grain. The IK research objectives in this case (Samanta and Prasad 1995) were to study the usefulness of the practice, to document in detail the operations involved, and to disseminate this information to other farmers. Scientists collected information from the farmers through discussions, personal observations, and open-ended questionnaires. Information was collected on the grain-storage process: the quantity of grain kept in the baskets or bins; the quantity of neem leaves used for a particular quantity of grain; the length of time the neem leaves were kept in the baskets; and the total time the grain remained in the containers. The scientists found that the quantity of grain stored in a basket varied from 50 to 100 kilograms. For every 50 kilograms of grain, 200 grams of neem leaves was added, together with a few tender branches. Through controlled trials, scientists reported that the grain stored with neem leaves was not affected by pests for 2–3 months, whereas grain stored without neem leaves was infested.

Puffer (1994) described an indigenous technology from Burkina Faso, where farmers used stone lines, in combination with pits, to curb soil erosion and to increase water infiltration and soil fertility. The sorghum yields in the fields with the IK technology were 40% greater than in fields without the technology.

IK experimentation

The transfer of IK technologies does not necessarily mean that IK is applied in its original form. A blend of local IK, IK from other localities, and Western science or other outside knowledge may yield very good results (for example, applying local pesticides with Western equipment to improve the distribution of a pesticide).

According to Warren and Rajasekaran (1993), the incorporation of IK systems into agricultural development has three components:

1 Participatory on-station agricultural research (scientists and farmers);

2 On-farm farmer-oriented research (scientists, extensionists, and farmers); and

3 Validation of farmer experiments (farmers and extensionists).

The first two components are sequenced, whereas the third is a separate process.

IIRR (1996) identified three components for improving IK:

• Formal research in laboratories and on experimental farms;

• On-farm research managed by scientists; and

• Farmer-managed participatory technology development.

Participatory on-station research

Research-station scientists can conduct research that builds on collected IK, with the participation of farmers who have a tendency to experiment on their own. As an example, farmers in India intercrop a multipurpose tree with some leguminous crops, but the legumes spread too quickly between the trees. The research-station scientists might conduct on-station experiments to evaluate the performance of various legume varieties, selecting legume varieties that are more suitable for intercropping. The successful combinations of tree, and legume varieties could then be used in on-farm farmer-oriented research, for validation under farmers' field conditions.

On-farm farmer-oriented research

To validate participatory on-station research, researchers (and farmers) can present technological options to selected farmers. Farmers can then choose an option based on their specific problems and resource constraints.

Each option can be compared using the Barometer of Sustainability. Another way to present the options to the farmers would be to use a matrix. The performance of various technological options can be presented against relevant criteria. A number of quantitative measures may now be available from the on-station experimental trials. For instance, let's say that the various (improved) technological options have slightly different impacts on soil fertility (ecosystem), cash requirements and yield (human needs), local practice (social), and women (equity). The likely advantages and disadvantages of each option can be presented to farmers. Farmers can then select one technology from a menu of (ecologically) sustainable options for testing on their entire farm, and this on-farm research will facilitate an in-depth understanding of the interactions among crops, trees, and livestock. The decision to test certain options must rest with the farmers, not with development workers or scientists.

Validation of farmer experiments

Conducting on-station and on-farm research has two potential limitations. First, bringing the researcher–extensionist–farmer community together is difficult. Second, depending entirely on research stations for innovations is impractical because of the limitations on available human resources. Thus, validation of the farmers' own experiments is an attractive alternative. Warren and Rajasekaran (1993) advocated using well-trained, research-minded extension personnel to

- Determine the rationale behind the farmers' experiments (for example, the farmer may be testing varieties for increases in yield or for local adaptation);

- Record the farmers' experimental methods (for example, some farmers conduct trials by raising local and high-yielding varieties in the same plot; others may use two different plots); and

- Identify the farmers' evaluation criteria (for example, the criteria may differ from farmer to farmer, or one farmer may have different criteria for different crops).

After the farmers' experiments have been validated, the extension personnel should conduct local and regional workshops to present the results. The research farmers should be involved as resource persons at these workshops. Farmers may conclude that the technological option(s) should be discarded, transferred, or researched in greater depth. Farmers can be compensated with cash prizes for their contribution to the development of technologies. Successful technologies can be promoted at other regional and national workshops.

Final comments

The previous sections introduced the topic of IK. The discussion included factors important to developing a research framework, such as research paradigms and issues that have influenced IK research practice. IPR, IUCN's planning framework, and insights from the social sciences and gender-sensitive and participatory rural research were discussed. Thirty-one techniques for data collection were introduced, followed by several case studies demonstrating a variety of research objectives and the use of some of the collection techniques. This last section dealt with assessing the product of IK research in terms of sustainability and developing IK through validation and experimentation. Appendix 1 provides three sets of formal procedural guidelines for conducting IK research: Inuit research guidelines, the Dene Cultural Institute guidelines, and some general rules and procedures for IK research from IIRR.

Sustainability will depend on improving and maintaining the well-being of people and their ecosystem. At the local level, the people–ecosystem combinations will reflect the development goals and choices of local people. This package of information provides a much needed synthesis of IK research and should convey IK's pivotal role in sustainable development. I wish you success in your own efforts to work *with* IK.

Sample Guidelines

Three sample guidelines for indigenous knowledge (IK) research are presented below. Each offers an "ideal" to guide an IK research process and some pathways to get to that ideal. Location-specific constraints may make it impossible to implement all the suggestions at a given location. Nevertheless, it is useful, and perhaps necessary, to keep the visions in mind. The Inuit research guidelines, developed by the Inuit Tapirisat of Canada, offer 12 principles for community-controlled research (ITC n.d.). The Dene Cultural Institute (DCI) guidelines outline some detailed procedures for a community-managed and -controlled research project. The International Institute of Rural Reconstruction (IIRR) guidelines offer some general rules and procedures for collecting, recording, and documenting IK.

Inuit research guidelines

Research principles for community-controlled research with the Inuit Tapirisat of Canada

1   Informed consent should be obtained from the community and from any individuals involved in research.

2   In seeking informed consent the researcher should at least explain the purpose of the research; sponsors of research; the person in charge; potential benefits and possible problems associated with the research for people and the environment; research methodology; participation of or contact with residents of the community.

3   Anonymity and confidentiality must be offered and, if accepted, guaranteed except where this is legally precluded.

4   Ongoing communication of research objectives, methods, findings and interpretation from inception to completion of project should occur.

5   If, during the research, the community decides the research is unacceptable, the research should be suspended.

6   Serious efforts must be made to include local and traditional knowledge in all stages of the research including problem identification.

7   Research design should endeavour to anticipate and provide meaningful training of aboriginal researchers.

8   Research must avoid social disruption.

9   Research must respect the privacy, dignity, cultures, traditions and rights of aboriginal people.

10 Written information should be available in the appropriate language(s).

11 The peer review process must be communicated to the communities, and their advice and/or participation sought in the process.

12 Aboriginal people should have access to research data, not just receive summaries and research reports. The extent of data accessibility that participants/ communities can expect should be clearly stated and agreed on as part of any approval process.

Dene Cultural Institute guidelines

The Dene people live in the Canadian Northwest. The DCI (1991) guidelines represent a gender-sensitive, participatory approach for conducting research to document traditional ecological knowledge. The guidelines address intellectual property rights and set the foundation for a cooperative research venture that will be mutually beneficial to the community and to the outside agency. Although these guidelines reflect the needs and aspirations of the Dene people, some aspects are adaptable for other cultural situations. (The DCI guidelines were lightly edited and reformatted for inclusion in this guidebook.)

Guidelines for the conduct of participatory community research to document traditional ecological knowledge for the purpose of environmental assessment and environmental management

1   Establishing cooperative research ventures: the development process

- *Identify the partner community and establish a cooperative research venture —* The first step is to identify the partner community and by consultation develop a joint agreement to carry out the project within parameters acceptable to both the community and the outside agency. This may require several meetings with local government and the community at large, during which the objectives, proposed research methodology, and expected results are thoroughly examined and explained in non-technical language. Before the signing of an agreement, the community should understand the commitments it would be expected to make and the benefits it could expect to receive. The community should also have the opportunity to add to or to modify the objectives of the research program before it is implemented. Although elected community representatives are the signatories of the cooperative agreement, the approval and support of the general community are essential to the project and should be obtained by consensus, if possible.

- *Establish a community administrative committee to oversee the direction and operation of the project —* Once the project is approved, the outside agency should consult with the local authorities to establish a permanent administrative committee in the community to direct and oversee the operation of the project. The committee members should include representatives from the community, identified by the local authorities, and one representative from the outside agency. The outsider would play only a supportive and advisory role to the committee and would liaise between the community and the outside agency. The responsibilities of the Community Administrative Committee include, inter alia, selecting project personnel, defining the duties and responsibilities of the various actors, project monitoring, and project administration.

- *Obtain approval of workplan and budget from the outside agency and establish a funding agreement and payment schedule —* Once the project's terms of reference, the various committees, a workplan, the criteria for selecting local and outside researchers, and a budget have been defined, the community should seek final approval from the sponsoring agency. Upon approval, the funds should be deposited in an account in the community. A local person with experience should take responsibility for the project accounting. If there is no one available in the community to carry out this responsibility, training should be provided.

- *Establish an Elders' Council of experts in the topic* — Because most traditional ecological knowledge is provided by the older community members, an Elders' Council would be an important asset for a community research program. This advisory body could provide valuable assistance in the interpretation of language and data, suggestions for areas of research that are important to pursue, and recommendations for the selection of community researchers. An Elders' Council would also help restore the traditional role of elders as community teachers and advisors, respected for their knowledge and wisdom. The Community Administrative Committee, in consultation with the local authorities and other knowledgeable community members, should select the Elders' Council.

- *Select community researchers* — The Community Administrative Committee, in consultation with the Elders' Council, should select the community researchers. One of the most important criteria in the selection of community researchers is the ability to communicate well in the local language and the outsider language. Without these skills, the work cannot be done effectively. The alternatives are to have an intensive language(s) training program for researchers, which may be too costly for individual projects, or to have a qualified interpreter work with the community researchers. Other important qualities are awareness of local traditional culture, previous research experience, interest, and motivation. On nearly all broad subjects of research, there will be some perspectives and knowledge that are generally held by women and some that are generally held by men. A mixed-gender research team presents an opportunity for discussing and dealing directly with gender issues and will help the team access all perspectives. If gender is an issue in the interviewing of some older men and women, it may be advisable to let the researchers of the same sex work with these individuals. It must also be recognized that the rapport established between the interviewer and the interviewee depends on many social and interpersonal factors that are unrelated to gender (for example, kinship and personality). The payment of community researchers and their work schedule (part time or full time) should be decided on by the Community Administrative Committee.

- *Select outside researchers* — The Community Administrative Committee should select any outside researchers the committee members feel would benefit the project. Outside researchers should offer advice and support to the community and to the local researchers. They should not be responsible for directing the research. Depending on the nature of the project and the experience of the community researchers, the outside researchers may be required to provide local training. In addition to their academic qualifications, it would help if the outside researchers had some previous hands-on experience living with the culture they will be working with and are prepared to participate in community life as much as possible during their stay. Although both outside and local researchers bring their own cultural biases and personal interests to any project, the credibility of the outside researchers will be enhanced if they are not perceived by the community as being closely aligned with government or nongovernment agencies, whose interests may be in conflict with those of the community. Outside researchers should remain in close contact with the local researchers throughout the project to provide them with guidance and feedback.

- *Select a technical advisory committee* — Where possible, a pool of resource people should be available to provide advice and feedback to the research team. Such an advisory committee should consist of professionals who are not aligned with the outside agency and who have extensive, relevant experience working in the different areas covered in the research (for example, a biologist, a social scientist, a linguist, individuals with previous experience in participatory community research or community development). These professionals would be called on to assist in the design of the research methodology and to provide help in the analysis and review of the final draft of the report.

- *Begin training program* — Community researchers in most cases will require some training to conduct the research. The type of training program provided to community researchers will depend on the type of project carried out, the individuals involved, and the time and money available to run it. For example, community researchers can be trained in interview techniques, questionnaire design, sampling, and data analysis. Any training program for doing research on traditional environmental knowledge should provide a good balance of field and classroom activities. Ideally, all or at least part of this training should take place in a field-camp setting and should include elders from the community, as instructors, as well as different scientists. This cross-cultural, interdisciplinary approach would permit local researchers to observe first hand the ecological topics under study, both from a Western scientific perspective and from an Aboriginal perspective. At the same time, scientists would have the opportunity to learn about traditional knowledge. A field-camp setting would also allow partici-pants, away from the distractions of everyday community life, to concentrate on learning. Depending on the language fluency of com-munity researchers, there might also be a need for intensive language instruction for both the community and the outside researcher. An important addition to any training program would be a basic linguis-tic component. This would help both the local and outside researchers understand and learn how to cope with the complexities of translation.

- *Select participants* — The Community Administrative Committee and the Elders' Council, in consultation with the local researchers, should select the participants. It is important to interview a wide range of participants to ensure that different perspectives are represented. The specific number of people to interview will depend on the availabil-ity of participants, the time frame of the project, and the information collected. The researchers can assume that they have sampled the range of information available when they stop seeing significant dif-ferences in responses. Although elders may be recognized as the most knowledgeable interviewees, it is worthwhile talking to middle-aged and young people (as well as rich and poor people). Also, it is impor-tant to interview both genders. Even if the research is focused on a technology used mainly by one gender, the other gender may still be very knowledgeable. They have heard the same stories and legends and have listened to discussions about these activities throughout their lives. One gender may also have specialized information. Often within a community, different individuals will be recognized as being partic-ularly knowledgeable about certain geographical areas or particular species. The Community Administrative Committee and the Elders' Council should decide how to pay the participants. Payment may be in the form of gifts or money. Informants can be paid an hourly wage for each interview, with a maximum amount for a whole day spent out on the land.

Traditional-knowledge research is a new and rapidly evolving field. There is no one correct method for data collection. Every project will have different objectives and limitations; hence, the methodology will have to be modified to suit individual needs. The key to successful research is to remain flexible and innovative in your study and to be sensitive to the needs and lifestyle of the community you are serving.

2   Developing the research methodology: retrieval and documentation of traditional ecological knowledge

- *Participant observation* — The ideal method for documenting and understanding traditional knowledge is participant observation, whereby a local researcher and a scientist work together as a team to interview informants in as natural a setting as possible (for example, while participating in relevant activities). The traditional activity, combined with the natural environment, provide a natural stimulus for discussion and learning for the scientist, the local researcher, and the informant. However, few projects have the time or the financial resources to use participant observation exclusively. Usually, the primary method of data collection is the ethnographic interview that uses a structured conversational approach; this should be supplemented by participant observation whenever possible.

- *Ethnographic interviews and structured and unstructured interviewing* — Given that community researchers are experienced or have received special training related to the project, the methods of questioning participants will vary among local researchers and the participants themselves. In some cases, the structured questionnaire, with its direct question and answer format, may be effective. In other instances, a more casual conversational approach may be most suitable. Some people require a lot of encouragement before they will talk. Others tend to wander off on subjects that may be irrelevant to the question, although saying what appears to be irrelevant may in fact be their way of answering the question (for example, through a story or legend). A lot depends on the interviewer's ability to sense when it is important to probe for more information or gently steer the conversation back on track. The more knowledgeable the interviewer is about the subject matter and the culture's way of expressing ideas, the more effective will be the interview.

- *Framing the questions* — Questions to obtain data that are important from a scientific perspective must be framed in culturally appropriate terms. Generally, it's better to avoid the use of scientific terms in questions, because they are often difficult to translate into the local language. There are also scientific concepts that, when translated, elicit a negative or confused response because they are culturally inappropriate ways of asking for that type of information. For example, the modern concept of wildlife management suggests the control of a species by humans. The idea of humans controlling the environment is considered by some indigenous groups to be an interference with the natural order, which from their cultural perspective is unacceptable. Another example is asking about the number of animals harvested. Some participants may be hesitant to reveal this type of information for fear that it might be used against them by the government. For others, talking about the number of harvested animals may be considered boasting. In both of these cases, local researchers can help design culturally appropriate questions.

- *Group, pair, and individual interviews* — Depending on the objective of the interview, either group, pair, or individual interviews may be used. Individual interviews allow the more reserved person to speak freely. On the other hand, some people may feel uncertain about the knowledge they have and be more at ease discussing their ideas in a group situation. In group interviews, unless the interviewer is very skilled at facilitating a group discussion, one or two people tend to dominate the interview, or the group breaks into smaller discussion groups. Group interviews are probably most useful for trying to get a consensus on a particular subject if there appears to be a wide range of opinions among respondents. Pair interviews are good because one person may help to jog the other's memory about a particular event or clarify a point. Often a husband and wife make a good team in this respect.

- *Recording the interview* — Wherever possible, all interviews should be recorded on (audio) tape. However, permission to tape-record must be given by the participant before the interview. Tape-recording allows the interviewer to concentrate on the questioning and to encourage the participant. However, not everyone may agree to be tape-recorded, in which case it may be better to have two people participate in the interview, one to ask the questions and the other to take notes. Even if the interview is being tape-recorded, it is always a good idea for the interviewer to take a few notes to clarify certain points at the end of the interview. Where applicable, some data should be recorded on maps of appropriate scale. Having a map of the area present during the interview may also help stimulate a participant to talk about a particular geographical area or species.

3   Conducting the interview

- *The setting of the interview* — Researchers should conduct interviews in places where the participant is most comfortable.

- *Preliminary interview* — Interviews should be preceded by a brief, informal discussion with the participant(s) to outline the purpose of the interview, to indicate the type of information sought, and to set the time and location of the formal interview. If a general policy regarding the control and use of the project data has not been established by the Community Administrative Committee, participants should be informed of their right to decide how the information from their interviews should be used. All participants should be required to sign a release form at the beginning of each interview. The release form should indicate who should have access to the information, beyond the use of the specific project (for example, the general public, only community members), and when they can have access to the information (for example, now, in 10 years, or when the informant is deceased).

- *Conducting the interview* — The most important step in conducting an interview is to put the participant at ease. (Local researchers in northern Canada have found that often the best approach is to begin the interview by having tea together.) During the interview, the interviewer should avoid asking leading questions and citing the names of persons who have provided contradictory opinions. The interviewer must make an effort to show interest in the conversation through eye contact and other responses. The interviewer should be sensitive to signs of fatigue, and if this becomes apparent, arrange to stop the interview and continue at another time. Most interviews should not last more than 2 hours.

- *Transcription and translation of interviews* — Transcribing and translating tapes are very time consuming. Community researchers should transcribe the tapes verbatim into the Aboriginal language as soon as the interview is completed. This way, the information is still fresh in their minds, and if there are any problems of interpretation the researcher can easily return to the participant to clarify points. This routine also prevents a backlog of tapes needing transcription. If the interviews are to be translated, community and outside researchers should work together to translate at least one interview per topic early on in the interviewing process to ensure that any problems of translation are resolved before the work gets too far along. It is important to fully understand the Aboriginal terms and concepts to ensure that the meaning is not lost or distorted in the translation. Once the transcriptions and translations of interviews are completed, community researchers should go over the contents with the participants to ensure correct interpretation. If there are major differences in responses among the participants about a particular subject, a meeting of the Elders' Council should be held to discuss the issue.

- *Analysis, organization, and management of data* — It is difficult to recommend a particular method of data analysis and management because each project will have specific objectives and methods of documentation. A few suggestions for analyzing and managing data that should have general application to other research on traditional ecological knowledge are offered. Information on traditional ecological knowledge for use by government administrators and the scientific community usually needs to be put into technical or scientific language to make it more meaningful and useful to these outside users. It is therefore advisable for the outside researcher to review the verbatim (translated) transcripts and to reinterpret and rewrite the data in appropriate language. The data are then analyzed and evaluated for completeness and relevance to the research objectives. Wherever possible, information from transcripts should be mapped. The base map will highlight information gaps and may identify potential conflicts.

- *Organization and storage of data* — Most traditional-knowledge information is presented in anecdotal form and is therefore difficult to classify and analyze. Often people will discuss several different subjects in answer to one question. Information can be classified according to different subjects and then summarized in nontechnical language.

- *Dissemination of information* — For the duration of the project, the Community Administrative Committee, the outside agency, and the community as a whole should be kept informed of the progress and of any major problems that arise. For the Community Administrative Committee and the outside agency, brief oral and written reports, supplemented with mapped and other graphic data, should suffice. Similar information may be presented to the community by talking about the project on the local radio or by holding an open house whereby the community can drop by the project office to talk with local and outside researchers. It is important to take photographs for displays and public presentations. Progress reports and a summary of the final report should be translated into the local language and distributed widely, through, for instance, a community newsletter. Depending on the nature of the project and the availability of funds, it might also be useful to produce a video of the work. This would be useful for public education, for school curriculum, and for professional presentations. In the preparation of the final report, each of the participating groups should have input into its design and content before it is finalized (that is, the Community Administrative Committee, the Elders' Council, the Technical Advisory Committee, and the local and outside researchers). A draft report should be distributed to the agency and other individuals for comment. Once the report is finalized, a community meeting should be held to present the final results of the project. Copies of the final report should be sent to the community, the sponsoring agency, and appropriate others for future reference.

International Institute of Rural Reconstruction guidelines

IIRR is a nongovernmental organization that aims to improve the quality of rural peoples' lives. It has extensive practical experience with development projects and IK research. Its suggested procedures (IIRR 1996, pp. 19–21) repeat some aspects from the Dene and Inuit guidelines and summarize some inputs from other parts of the guidebook. One point that differentiates these guidelines from the Dene guidelines is that outside researchers define the research goals and objectives.

Rules and procedures when collecting, recording, and documenting IK

Preparations

- Define your study objectives.

- Determine content and extent of the study: What do you need to know? How much do you need to know? Do not attempt to collect more data than necessary!

Dos and don'ts of community work

- Don't force people to participate in the process.
- Don't be impatient.
- Don't ask a lot of questions all at once.
- Let people finish what they have to say and then ask your questions.
- Listen attentively and learn.
- Don't disturb ongoing discussions.
- When people are discussing one subject, don't introduce another.
- Include fence sitters (those who watch but do not actively participate).
- Be wary of people who dominate discussions. Deal with them diplomatically.
- When people discuss among themselves, do not try to influence them.
- Don't show approval or disapproval.
- Don't exchange signs between team members during discussions.
- Learn and use the local language.

Source: SHOGORIP (1992), cited in IIRR (1996, p. 21)

- Select methods for recording and documentation. Methods should yield the required information; be low-cost; be easily understood by community members; be fun; and place importance on local people rather than the researcher and other outsiders.

- Prepare for each method thoroughly before going to the community. If several people are involved, divide the work and agree on who will do what.

- Collect as much relevant information as you can about the community and related topics before you enter the community.

- Obtain permission from the community before you start the study or project.

Entering the community

- Introduce yourself and other outsiders to all community members involved.

- Explain to the community, in detail, the study or project objectives. Do not raise false expectations.

- Let people know that you have come to learn from them.

- Discuss with the community the possible benefits of the study.

- Inform community members of how much of their time the study will take.

- Learn the meaning of local terms.

- If possible, learn to speak the local language. This makes fieldwork much easier and is usually highly appreciated.

Learning about IK

- Ask neutral questions. Do not ask leading questions. Ask "What do you use this for?", rather than "Do you use this for cooking?"

- Use these words and phrases often: What? How? Why? Who? When? Where? How often? Where did you learn this?

- Listen. Observe.

- Be open. Try to achieve an insider's perspective.

- Keep alive the interest of local participants — know when to stop.

- Follow the dos and don'ts of community work.

Recording IK

- Record all information, even if it does not make sense from an outsider's point of view.

- Record as neutrally and in a manner as value free as possible. Record "Farmers use local breeds," rather than "Farmers still use local breeds."

When the study is finished

- Validate the output with the community.

- Provide the community with a copy of the output.

- Discuss how results will be used and how they can benefit the community.

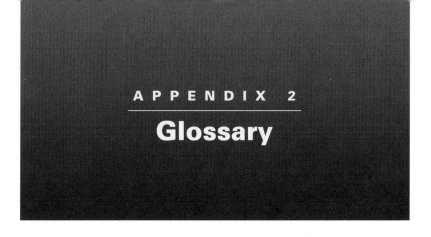

APPENDIX 2

Glossary

Biodiversity: All living organisms, their genetic material, and their ecosystems. Biodiversity encompasses genetic, specific, and ecosystem diversity (Posey and Dutfield 1996).

Biotechnology: Techniques that involve the use and manipulation of living organisms to make or modify products (Posey and Dutfield 1996).

Emic: The perspective of an insider for a given cultural phenomenon (Warren [1997]).

Etic: The perspective of an outsider for a given cultural phenomenon (Warren [1997]).

Gender: Our identity as women and men — refers to the characteristics, roles, and values that a specific culture has determined to be feminine or masculine (Durno and Chanyapate 1995).

Genetic engineering: Closely related to biotechnology, genetic engineering is a high-tech process in which specific genes from one organism are moved into another organism, introducing new characteristics into plants, animals, and microorganisms (SWGGS 1995a).

Germplasm: The total genetic variability, represented by germ cells or seeds, available to a particular population of organisms (RAFI 1996a).

Indigenous knowledge: Used synonymously with traditional and local knowledge to differentiate the knowledge developed by a given community from the knowledge generated through universities, government research centres, and private industry (the international knowledge system, sometimes called the Western system) (Warren 1992).

Intellectual property rights: Laws that grant monopoly rights to those who create ideas or knowledge. They are intended to protect inventors against losing control of their ideas or the creations of their knowledge. The five major forms of intellectual property rights — patents, plant-breeders' rights, copyright, trademarks, and trade secrets — operate by exclusion, granting temporary monopoly rights that prevent others from making or using the creation. Intellectual property legislation is national, although most countries adhere to international conventions governing intellectual property (RAFI 1996a).

Sustainable development: Development that meets the needs of the present without compromising the ability of future generations to meet their own needs (WCED 1997).

Technology: Hardware (equipment, tools, instruments, and energy sources) and software (a combination of knowledge, processes, skills, and social organizations) that focus attention on particular tasks (Massaquoi 1993).

Traditional ecological knowledge: The ability of Aboriginal peoples to comprehend local-ecosystem interrelationships and to achieve sustainable levels of resource use with no or minimum disruptions to ecosystem functions (AINA and JS–IRRC 1996).

APPENDIX 3

Acronyms and Abbreviations

FAO	Food and Agriculture Organization of the United Nations
GATT	General Agreement on Tariffs and Trade
HGDP	Human Genome Diversity Project
IDRC	International Development Research Centre
IIRR	International Institute of Rural Reconstruction
IK	indigenous knowledge
IPR	intellectual property rights
ITA	information-transfer agreement
IUCN	International Union for the Conservation of Nature and Natural Resources
MTA	material-transfer agreement
NGO	nongovernmental organization
PRA	participatory rural appraisal
RRA	rapid rural appraisal
TNC	transnational corporation
TRIPs	Trade-Related Aspects of Intellectual Property Rights
UCD	University of California at Davis
WTO	World Trade Organization

References

Abbink, J. 1995. Medicinal and ritual plants of the Ethiopian Southwest: an account of recent research. Indigenous Knowledge and Development Monitor, 3(2). Online: http://www.nufficcs.nl/ciran/ikdm/.

Adugna, G. 1996. The dynamics of knowledge systems vs. sustainable development: a sequel to the debate. Indigenous Knowledge and Development Monitor, 4(2). Online: http://www.nufficcs.nl/ciran/ikdm/.

Agrawal, A. 1993. Removing ropes, attaching strings: institutional arrangements to provide water. Indigenous Knowledge and Development Monitor, 1(3). Online: http://www.nufficcs.nl/ciran/ikdm/.

AINA; JS–IRRC (Arctic Institute of North America; Joint Secretariat–Inuvialuit Renewable Resource Committees). 1996. Circumpolar aboriginal people and co-management practice: current issues in co-management and environmental assessment. Arctic Institute of North America, Calgary, AB, Canada. 172 pp.

Appleton, H.E.; Hill, C.L.M. 1995. Gender and indigenous knowledge in various organizations. Indigenous Knowledge and Development Monitor, 2(3). Online: http://www.nufficcs.nl/ciran/ikdm/.

Baines, G.; Hviding, E. 1992. Traditional environmental knowledge from the Marovo area of the Solomon Islands. In Johnson, M., ed., Lore: capturing traditional environmental knowledge. Dene Cultural Institute; International Development Research Centre, Ottawa, ON, Canada. pp. 91–110.

Barker, R.; Cross, N. 1992. Documenting oral history in the African Sahel. In Johnson, M., ed., Lore: capturing traditional environmental knowledge. Dene Cultural Institute; International Development Research Centre, Ottawa, ON, Canada. pp. 113–140.

Benfer, R.A., Jr; Furbee, L. 1996. Can indigenous knowledge be brokered without scientific understanding of the community structure and distribution of that knowledge? A sequel to the debate (8). Indigenous Knowledge and Development Monitor, 4(2). Online: http://www.nufficcs.nl/ciran/ikdm/.

Berkes, F. 1993. Traditional ecological knowledge in perspective. *In* Inglis, J., ed., Traditional ecological knowledge: concepts and cases. International Program on Traditional Ecological Knowledge; International Development Research Centre, Ottawa, ON, Canada. pp. 1–9.

Brookfield, M. 1996. Indigenous knowledge: a long history and an uncertain future: a sequel to the debate (9). Indigenous Knowledge and Development Monitor, 4(2). Online: http://www.nufficcs.nl/ciran/ikdm/.

Capra, F. 1982. The turning point. Simon and Schuster, New York, NY, USA.

Chambers, R. 1992. Rural appraisal: rapid, relaxed and participatory. Institute for Development Studies, University of Sussex, Falmer, Brighton, UK. Discussion Paper No. 311.

Cimi (Indianist Missionary Council). 1997. Law may expel foreign research missions. Cimi, Brasilia, Brazil.

Conway, K. 1997. Improving crop resistance: a new plant breeding technique borrows from the past. IDRC Reports, 2 May 1997. Online: http://www.idrc.ca/books/reports/1997/17-01e.html.

CS Canada (Cultural Survival Canada). 1995. Indigenous peoples, biodiversity, and health. Cultural Survival Canada, Ottawa, ON, Canada. Factsheet, November.

────── 1996a. Indigenous peoples & intellectual property rights: responses from three regions. Cultural Survival Canada, Ottawa, ON, Canada. Factsheet, July.

────── 1996b. Is there a gene for the wetiko disease? Cultural Survival Canada, Ottawa, ON, Canada. Survival Update, Summer.

────── 1996c. The reinvention of slavery in biocolonial times. Cultural Survival Canada, Ottawa, ON, Canada. Survival Update, March.

────── 1996d. Toward biodiversity rights: the Convention on Biological Diversity and indigenous peoples. Cultural Survival Canada, Ottawa, ON, Canada. Discussion Paper, June.

Davidman, M. 1996. Creating, patenting and marketing of new forms of life. Community Economics, Multinational Operations. Online: http://www/demon. co.uk/solbaram/indexes/communi.html.

Davis, D.K. 1995. Gender-based differences in the ethnoveterinary knowledge of Afghan nomadic pastoralists. Indigenous Knowledge and Development Monitor, 3(1). Online: http://www.nufficcs.nl/ciran/ikdm/.

Dawkins, K.; Thom, M.; Carr, C. 1995. Intellectual property rights and biodiversity. Institute for Agriculture and Trade Policy, Minneapolis, MN, USA. Online: http://www.igc.org/iatp/ipr-info.html.

DCI (Dene Cultural Institute). 1991. Guidelines for the conduct of participatory community research to document traditional ecological knowledge for the purpose of environmental assessment and environmental management. Canadian Environmental Assessment Research Council, Hull, PQ, Canada. 38 pp.

de Vreede, M. 1996. Identification of land degradation levels at the grassroots. *In* Hambly, H.; Onweng Angura, T., ed., Grassroots indicators for desertification: experience and perspectives from eastern and southern Africa. International Development Research Centre, Ottawa, ON, Canada. pp. 75–82.

Doubleday, N.C. 1993. Finding common ground: natural law and collective wisdom. *In* Inglis, J., ed., Traditional ecological knowledge: concepts and cases. International Program on Traditional Ecological Knowledge; International Development Research Centre, Ottawa, ON, Canada. pp. 41–53.

Durning, A.B. 1989. Poverty and the environment: reversing the downward spiral. Worldwatch Institute, Washington, DC, USA. Worldwatch Paper No. 92.

Durno, J.; Chanyapate, C. 1995. Gender issues in sustainable development. *In* McGrath, P., ed., Sustainable development: voices from rural Asia, Vol. 1. Studio Driya Media; Canadian University Service Overseas, Bandung, Indonesia. pp. 94–96.

Emery, A.R. 1997. Guidelines for environmental assessments and traditional knowledge. Canadian International Development Agency; Environment Canada; Alan R. Emery & Associates, Ottawa, ON, Canada. A Report from the Centre for Traditional Knowledge to the World Council of Indigenous People. Prototype document.

Eythorsson, E. 1993. Sami fjord fishermen and the state: traditional knowledge and resource management in northern Norway. *In* Inglis, J., ed., Traditional ecological knowledge: concepts and cases. International Program on Traditional Ecological Knowledge; International Development Research Centre, Ottawa, ON, Canada. pp. 133–142.

Fernandez, P.G. 1994. Indigenous seed practices for sustainable development. Indigenous Knowledge and Development Monitor, 2(2). Online: http://www. nufficcs.nl/ciran/ikdm/.

Fujisaka, S.; Jayson, E.; Dapusala, A. 1993. 'Recommendation domain' and a farmers' upland rice technology. Indigenous Knowledge and Development Monitor, 1(3). Online: http://www.nufficcs.nl/ciran/ikdm/.

FWIIIS (Four Worlds International Institute for Indigenous Sciences). 1995–96. Summary. Four Directions International Inc., Lethbridge, AB, Canada. Online: http://www.nucleus.com/4worlds/fwiiois.html.

Gadgil, M.; Berkes, F.; Folke, C. 1993. Indigenous knowledge for biodiversity conservation. Ambio, 22(2–3), 151–156.

Glassman, J. 1994. GATT and retail food association. Institute for Agriculture and Trade Policy, Minneapolis, MN, USA. Online: http://www.igc.org/iatp/ipr-info.html.

Global 2000. 1997. European Parliament signals go-ahead for corporate control of life? Global 2000, Brussels, Belgium.

Grandstaff, S.W.; Grandstaff, T.B. 1987. Semi-structured interviewing by multidisciplinary teams in RRA. *In* Proceedings of the 1985 International Conference on Rapid Rural Appraisal. Rural Systems Research and Farming Systems Research Projects, Khon Kaen University, Thailand. pp. 129–143.

Gupta, A.K. 1997. "Biopiracy" vis-à-vis gene fund: a novel experiment in benefit sharing. Honey Bee, 8(2).

Hanyani-Mlambo, B.T.; Hebinck, P. 1996. Formal and informal knowledge networks in conservation forestry in Zimbabwe. Indigenous Knowledge and Development Monitor, 4(3). Online: http://www.nufficcs.nl/ciran/ikdm/.

Harry, D. 1995a. The Human Genome Diversity Project and its implications for indigenous peoples. Institute for Agriculture and Trade Policy, Minneapolis, MN, USA. Online: http://www.igc.org/iatp/ipr-info.html.

——— 1995b. Patenting of life and its implications for indigenous peoples. Institute for Agriculture and Trade Policy, Minneapolis, MN, USA. Online: http://www. igc.org/iatp/ipr-info.html.

Hatch, J.K. 1976. Peasants who write a textbook on subsistence farming practices in northern coastal Peru. Land Tenure Center, University of Wisconsin, Madison, WI, USA. Monograph No. 1.

Hinton, R. 1995. Trades in different worlds: listening to refugee voices. *In* PLA notes, notes on participatory learning and action. No. 24: Critical reflections from practice. Sustainable Agriculture Programme, International Institute for Environment and Development, London, UK. pp. 21–26.

Hunter, D. 1996. Traditional pest control and agricultural development in the atolls of the Maldives. Indigenous Knowledge and Development Monitor, 4(3). Online: http://www.nufficcs.nl/ciran/ikdm/.

IIED (International Institute for Environment and Development). 1994. RRA notes. No. 21: Special issue on participatory tools and methods in urban areas. Sustainable Agriculture Programme and Human Settlements Programme, IIED, London, UK. 100 pp.

———— 1995. PLA notes, notes on participatory learning and action. No. 24: Critical reflections from practice. Sustainable Agriculture Programme, IIED, London, UK. 90 pp.

IIRR (International Institute of Rural Reconstruction). 1996. Recording and using indigenous knowledge: a manual. IIRR, Cavite, Philippines. 211 pp.

ITC (Inuit Tapirisat of Canada). n.d. Research principles for community-controlled research with the Tapirisat Inuit of Canada. Inuit Tapirisat of Canada, Ottawa, ON, Canada. 1 p.

IUCN (International Union for the Conservation of Nature and Natural Resources). 1997. An approach to assessing progress toward sustainability — tools and training series. IUCN Publication Services Unit, Cambridge, UK.

Jain, S.K.; Lahta, S. 1996. Unique indigenous Amazonian uses of some plants growing in India. Indigenous Knowledge and Development Monitor, 4(3). Online: http://www.nufficcs.nl/ciran/ikdm/.

Johannes, R.E. 1993. Integrating traditional ecological knowledge and management with environmental impact assessment. *In* Inglis, J., ed., Traditional ecological knowledge: concepts and cases. International Program on Traditional Ecological Knowledge; International Development Research Centre, Ottawa, ON, Canada. pp. 33–39.

Johnson, M. 1992. Research on traditional environmental knowledge: its development and its role. *In* Johnson, M., ed., Lore: capturing traditional environmental knowledge. Dene Cultural Institute; International Development Research Centre, Ottawa, ON, Canada. pp. 3–22.

Kakonge, J.O. 1995. Traditional African values and their use in implementing Agenda 21. Indigenous Knowledge and Development Monitor, 3(2). Online: http://www. nufficcs.nl/ciran/ikdm/.

Kater, A. 1993. Indigenous learning in crafts: a pilot research effort. Indigenous Knowledge and Development Monitor, 1(1). Online: http://www. nufficcs.nl/ciran/ikdm/.

Kinyunyu, L.; Swantz, M.-L. 1996. Research methodologies for identifying and validating grassroots indicators. *In* Hambly, H.; Onweng Angura, T., ed., Grassroots indicators for desertification: experience and perspectives from eastern and southern Africa. International Development Research Centre, Ottawa, ON, Canada. pp. 60–74.

Kipuri, N. 1996. Pastoral Maasai grassroots indicators for sustainable resource management. *In* Hambly, H.; Onweng Angura, T., ed., Grassroots indicators for desertification: experience and perspectives from eastern and southern Africa. International Development Research Centre, Ottawa, ON, Canada. pp. 110–119.

Kothari, B. 1995. From oral to written: the documentation of knowledge in Ecuador. Indigenous Knowledge and Development Monitor, 3(2). Online: http://www. nufficcs.nl/ciran/ikdm/.

Kroma, S. 1996. The science of Pacific Island peoples. Indigenous Knowledge and Development Monitor, 4(2). Online: http://www.nufficcs.nl/ciran/ikdm/.

Krugmann, H. 1996. Toward improved indicators to measure desertification and monitor the implementation of the Desertification Convention. *In* Hambly, H.; Onweng Angura, T., ed., Grassroots indicators for desertification: experience and perspectives from eastern and southern Africa. International Development Research Centre, Ottawa, ON, Canada. pp. 20–37.

Laghi, B. 1997. Getting into the spirit of things. The Globe and Mail, 9 Aug 1997, pp. D1–D2.

Langendijk, M.A.M. 1996. Incorporating local knowledge into development action: an NGO in Pakistan; a sequel to the debate. Indigenous Knowledge and Development Monitor, 4(2). Online: http://www. nufficcs.nl/ciran/ikdm/.

Lehman, K. 1994. Pirates of diversity: the global threat to the Earth's seeds. Institute for Agriculture and Trade Policy, Minneapolis, MN, USA. Online: http://www. igc.org/iatp/ipr-info.html.

Loevinsohn, M.; Sperling, L. 1995. Joining on-farm conservation to development. Using Diversity Workshop, New Delhi, India, 19–21 Jun 1995. Report.

Lovelace, G. 1984. Cultural beliefs and the management of agro-ecosystems. *In* Rambo, T; Sajise, P.E., ed., An introduction to human ecology research on agricultural systems in South East Asia. East–West Centre, Honolulu, HI, USA. pp. 194–205.

MacMillan, N. 1995. Andean farming for present and future. IDRC Reports, 25 Sep. Online: http://www.idrc.ca/books/reports/09highla.html.

MacPherson, N.; Netro, G. 1989. Community impact assessment: the community of Old Crow, Yukon. Canadian Environmental Assessment Research Council, Hull, PQ, Canada. 36 pp.

Mascarenhas, J.; Shah, P.; Joseph, S.; Jayakaran, R.; Devavaram, J.; Ramachandran, V.; Fernancez, A.; Chambers, R.; Pretty, J., ed. 1991. Proceedings of the February 1991 Bangalore PRA trainers workshop. International Institute for Environment and Development, London, UK.

Massaquoi, J.G.M. 1993. Indigenous technology for off-farm rural activities. Indigenous Knowledge and Development Monitor, 1(3). Online: http://www.nufficcs.nl/ciran/ikdm/.

Matowanyika, J.Z. 1991. Indigenous resource management and sustainability in rural Zimbabwe: an exploration of practices and concepts in commonlands. Department of Geography, University of Waterloo, Waterloo, ON, Canada. PhD thesis.

Maundu, P. 1995. Methodology for collecting and sharing indigenous knowledge: a case study. Indigenous Knowledge and Development Monitor, 3(2). Online: http://www.nufficcs.nl/ciran/ikdm/.

Mazzucato, V. 1997. Indigenous economies: bridging the gap between economics and anthropology. Indigenous Knowledge and Development Monitor, 5(1). Online: http://www.nufficcs.nl/ciran/ikdm/.

McCorkle, C.A. 1989. Towards a knowledge of local knowledge and its importance for agriculture RD&E. Agriculture and Human Values, 6(3), 4–11.

Meister, I; Mayer, S. 1995. Releases of genetically engineered plants and their impacts on less developed countries. Institute for Agriculture and Trade Policy, Minneapolis, MN, USA. Online: http://www.igc.org/iatp/ipr-info.html.

Melnyk, M. 1995. The contribution of forest foods to the livelihoods of the Piaroa Amerindians of southern Venezuela. Indigenous Knowledge and Development Monitor, 3(2). Online: http://www.nufficcs.nl/ciran/ikdm/.

Mosse, D. 1994. Authority, gender and knowledge: theoretical reflections on the practice of participatory rural appraisal. Development and Change, 25, 497–526.

Mwadime, R.K.N. 1996. Changes in environmental conditions: their potential as indicators for monitoring household food security. *In* Hambly, H.; Onweng Angura, T., ed., Grassroots indicators for desertification: experience and perspectives from eastern and southern Africa. International Development Research Centre, Ottawa, ON, Canada. pp. 85–94.

Mwesigye, F. 1996. Language and grassroots environment indicators. *In* Hambly, H.; Onweng Angura, T., ed., Grassroots indicators for desertification: experience and perspectives from eastern and southern Africa. International Development Research Centre, Ottawa, ON, Canada. pp. 55–59.

Mwinyimbegu, K.S. 1996. Research and training directed toward the conservation of IK: the training of local people; a sequel to the debate.

Indigenous Knowledge and Development Monitor, 4(2). Online: http://www.nufficcs.nl/ciran/ikdm/.

Nakashima, D.J. 1990. Application of native knowledge in EIA: Inuit, eiders and Hudson Bay oil. Canadian Environmental Assessment Research Council, Hull, PQ, Canada. 27 pp.

Narayan, D. 1996. Toward participatory research. World Bank, Washington, DC, USA. Technical Paper No. 307. 265 pp.

Nowlan, L.C. 1995. Bioprospecting or biopiracy? West Coast Environmental Law Newsletter, 19(10). Online: http://freenet.vancouver.bc.ca/localpages/wcel/4976/1.

Oduol, W. 1996. Akamba land management systems: the role of grassroots indicators in drought-prone cultures. *In* Hambly, H.; Onweng Angura, T., ed., Grassroots indicators for desertification: experience and perspectives from eastern and southern Africa. International Development Research Centre, Ottawa, ON, Canada. pp. 95–104.

Pahlman, C. 1995. Perceptions — Thailand: "soil erosion? — that's not how we see the problem!" *In* McGrath, P., ed., Sustainable development: voices from rural Asia, Vol. 1. Studio Driya Media; Canadian University Service Overseas, Bandung, Indonesia. pp. 75–79.

Posey, D.A.; Dutfield, G. 1996. Beyond intellectual property: toward traditional resource rights for indigenous peoples and local communities. International Development Research Centre, Ottawa, ON, Canada. 303 pp.

Puffer, P. 1994. Agricultural innovations from developing countries. Iowa Agriculturist, Fall issue, pp. 20–22.

——— 1995. The value of indigenous knowledge in development programs concerning Somali pastoralists and their camels. Iowa State University, IA, USA. 8 pp.

RAFI (Rural Advancement Foundation International) 1995. Utility plant patents: a review of the U.S. experience. RAFI, Ottawa, ON, Canada. Communiqué, Jul–Aug.

——— 1996a. Enclosures of the mind: intellectual monopolies. A resource kit on community knowledge, biodiversity and intellectual property. RAFI, Ottawa, ON, Canada. 79 pp.

——— 1996b. The geopolitics of biodiversity: a biodiversity balance sheet. RAFI, Ottawa, ON, Canada. Communiqué, Jan–Feb.

Richards, P. 1980. Community environmental knowledge. *In* Brokensha, D.W; Warren, D.M; Werner, O., ed., Indigenous knowledge systems and development. University Press of America, Lahham, MD, USA. pp.183–196.

Ruddle, K. 1993. The transmission of traditional ecological knowledge. *In* Inglis, J., ed., Traditional ecological knowledge: concepts and cases. International Program on Traditional Ecological Knowledge; International Development Research Centre, Ottawa, ON, Canada. pp. 17–31.

Sallenave, J. 1994. Giving traditional ecological knowledge its rightful place in environmental impact assessment. CARC — Northern Perspectives, 22(1).

Samanta, R.K.; Prasad, M.V. 1995. An indigenous post-harvest technology. Indigenous Knowledge and Development Monitor, 3(2). Online: http://www.nufficcs.nl/ciran/ikdm/.

Satterthwaite, A.J. 1997. Public voices and wilderness in environmental assessment: a philosophical analysis of resource policy decisions. Faculty of Environmental Studies, York University, North York, ON, Canada. PhD thesis.

Sayeed, A.T. 1994. GATT and Third World pharmaceuticals. Institute for Agriculture and Trade Policy, Minneapolis, MN. Online: http://www.igc.org/iatp/ipr-info.html.

Shankar, D. 1996. The epistemology of the indigenous medical knowledge systems of India. Indigenous Knowledge and Development Monitor, 4(3). Online: http://www.nufficcs.nl/ciran/ikdm/.

Shiva, V. 1995a. Biodiversity, biotechnology and profits. *In* McGrath, P., ed., Sustainable development: voices from rural Asia, Vol. 1. Studio Driya Media; Canadian University Service Overseas, Bandung, Indonesia. pp. 63–68.

————— 1995b. Patents, intellectual property and the politics of knowledge. *In* McGrath, P., ed., Sustainable development: voices from rural Asia, Vol. 1. Studio Driya Media; Canadian University Service Overseas, Bandung, Indonesia. pp. 69–71.

SHOGORIP. 1992. PRA guidelines: a manual to support PRA activities in Bangladesh. SHOGORIP, Bangladesh.

Simpson, B.M. 1994. Gender and the social differentiation of local knowledge. Indigenous Knowledge and Development Monitor, 2(3). Online: http://www.nufficcs.nl/ciran/ikdm/.

Soleri, D.; Cleaveland, D. 1993. Seeds of strength for Hopis and Zunis. Seedling, 10(4), 13–18.

Stone, L.; Campbell, J.G. 1984. The use and misuse of surveys in international development: an experiment from Nepal. Human Organization, 43(1), 27–37.

SWGGS (Shiva Working Group on Global Sustainability). 1995a. Genetic engineering. Institute for Agriculture and Trade Policy, Minneapolis, MN, USA. Online: http://www.igc.org/iatp/ipr-info.html.

——— 1995b. A primer on agricultural biotechnology. Institute for Agriculture and Trade Policy, Minneapolis, MN, USA. Online: http://www.igc.org/iatp/ipr-info. html.

Thrupp, L.A. 1989. Legitimizing local knowledge: from displacement to empowerment for Third World people. Agriculture and Human Values, 6(3), 13–24.

Titilola, T. 1995. IKS and sustainable agricultural development in Africa: essential linkages. Indigenous Knowledge and Development Monitor, 2(2). Online: http://www. nufficcs.nl/ciran/ikdm/.

Van Crowder, L. 1996. A sequel to the debate (3). Indigenous Knowledge and Development Monitor, 4(2). Online: http://www.nufficcs.nl/ciran/ikdm/.

von Geusau, L.A.; Wongprasert, S.; Trakansupakon, P. 1992. Regional development in northern Thailand: its impact on highlanders. *In* Johnson, M., ed., Lore: capturing traditional environmental knowledge. Dene Cultural Institute; International Development Research Centre, Ottawa, ON, Canada. pp. 143–163.

Warren, M.D. 1992. Indigenous knowledge, biodiversity conservation and development: keynote address. International Conference on Conservation of Biodiversity in Africa: Local Initiatives and Institutional Roles, 30 Aug – 3 Sep, Nairobi, Kenya. National Museums of Kenya, Nairobi, Kenya. 15 pp.

——— [1997]. Indigenous knowledge and education project — CIKARD; Bono therapeutics in Ghana. Center for Indigenous Knowledge for Agriculture and Rural Development, Iowa State University, IA, USA. Online: http://www.physics.iastate.edu/cikard/bono.htm.

Warren, M.D.; Rajasekaran, B. 1993. Putting local knowledge to good use. International Agricultural Development, 13(4), 8–10.

Wavey, R. 1993. International Workshop on Indigenous Knowledge and Community-based Resource Management: keynote address. *In* Inglis, J., ed., Traditional ecological knowledge: concepts and cases. International Program on Traditional Ecological Knowledge; International Development Research Centre, Ottawa, ON, Canada. pp. 11–16.

Wickham, T.W. 1993. Farmers ain't no fools: exploring the role of participatory rural appraisal to access indigenous knowledge and enhance sustainable development research and planning. A case study of Dusun

Pausan, Bali, Indonesia. Faculty of Environmental Studies, University of Waterloo, Waterloo, ON, Canada. Master's thesis. 211 pp.

Wilk, R. 1995. Sustainable development: practical, ethical, and social issues in technology transfer in traditional technology for environmental conservation and sustainable development in the Asian-Pacific region. Proceedings, UNESCO–University of Tsukuba International Seminar on Traditional Technology for Environmental Conservation and Sustainable Development in the Asian-Pacific Region, 11–14 Dec, Tsukuba Science City, Japan. United Nations Educational, Scientific and Cultural Organization, New York, NY, USA; University of Tsukuba, Tsukuba, Japan. 21 pp.

Wolfe, J.; Bechard, C.; Cizek, P.; Cole, D. 1992. Indigenous and Western knowledge and resource management systems. University of Guelph, Guelph, ON, Canada. Rural Reportings, Native Canadian Issues Series, No.1.

WCED (World Commission on Environment and Development). 1987. Our common future. Oxford University Press, New York, NY, USA.

Zwahlen, R. 1996. Traditional methods: a guarantee for sustainability? Indigenous Knowledge and Development Monitor, 4(3). Online: http://www.nufficcs.nl/ciran/ikdm/.

Zweifel, H. 1997. Biodiversity and the appropriation of women's knowledge. Indigenous Knowledge and Development Monitor, 5(1). Online: http://www.nufficcs.nl/ciran/ikdm/.

The Author

Louise Grenier received her degree in environmental studies from York University in 1990. Since then, she has worked on environmental and indigenous-knowledge issues with the University of Indonesia, the Institute of Technology (Bandung, Indonesia), UNESCO, the ING Coalition, IDRC, and the Nunavut Impact Review Board Transition Team, where, among other duties, she provided research, advice, and technical support on how to integrate traditional knowledge into the environmental assessment process. Her expertise is in designing, implementing, and managing research and training activities that focus on equity, sustainability, and sound environmental practice.

About the Institution

The International Development Research Centre (IDRC) is committed to building a sustainable and equitable world. IDRC funds developing-world researchers, thus enabling the people of the South to find their own solutions to their own problems. IDRC also maintains information networks and forges linkages that allow Canadians and their developing-world partners to benefit equally from a global sharing of knowledge. Through its actions, IDRC is helping others to help themselves.

About the Publisher

IDRC BOOKS publishes research results and scholarly studies on global and regional issues related to sustainable and equitable development. As a specialist in development literature, IDRC BOOKS contributes to the body of knowledge on these issues to further the cause of global understanding and equity. IDRC publications are sold through its head office in Ottawa, Canada, as well as by IDRC's agents and distributors around the world.